M000251039

Designing for the Homeless

Designing for the Homeless

ARCHITECTURE THAT WORKS

Sam Davis

UNIVERSITY OF CALIFORNIA PRESS Berkeley Los Angeles London

University of California Press
Berkeley and Los Angeles, California

University of California Press, Ltd.
London, England

Library of Congress Cataloging-in-Publication Data

Davis, Sam, 1946–
Designing for the homeless : architecture that works / Sam Davis.
p. cm.
Includes bibliographical references and index.
ISBN 0-520-23525-8 (cloth : alk. paper)
1. Public housing—United States. 2. Architecture, Domestic—United States. 3. Shelters for the homeless—United States. 4. Homeless persons—Housing. I. Title.
NA7540.D385 2004
728'.31'086942—dc22 2004005550

Manufactured in the United States of America

13 12 11 10 09 08 07 06 05
10 9 8 7 6 5 4 3 2

The paper used in this publication meets the minimum requirements of ANSI/NISO Z39.48–1992 (R 1997) *(Permanence of Paper)*.

The publisher gratefully acknowledges the generous contribution to this book provided by the Harriett Gold Architecture, Art, and Design Endowment Fund of the University of California Press Associates.

CONTENTS

PREFACE

I HAD BEEN DESIGNING affordable housing for thirty years when, in 1995, I began a project for the Larkin Street Youth Services, a nonprofit organization that serves homeless youth in San Francisco. The Larkin Street group wanted me to design housing for homeless teenagers and young adults who were HIV-positive or who had AIDS. Before I started the project, I regarded homelessness as one aspect of the San Francisco Bay Area's housing affordability crisis—that is, as a social, economic, and political issue—rather than as a design problem requiring the services of an architect. I came to understand, however, that the shortage of affordable housing is not the only problem facing many of the homeless. Without a place to call home, they are denied many other necessities, opportunities, and choices. Most important, perhaps, it is difficult to get or keep a job if one has no permanent address or telephone number and no place to shower, launder clothing, or store clean clothes. Homelessness also complicates access to health care, legal assistance, and education, and it restricts even such simple choices as when, where, and what to eat.

As I continued to work with nonprofit emergency housing and service providers on the design of shelters and facilities for the homeless, I came to appreciate how much even small gestures of thoughtful design can accomplish. At its most basic, designing a shelter entails fitting the requisite number of beds in a given space. But my clients and I have moved beyond logistics to explore how design can help establish trust between the provider and the homeless and how design can create a sense of belonging for people who may have few social connections. Good design also benefits the staff who work with the homeless. These remarkably generous people earn less-than-generous pay for long hours in stressful and difficult jobs, and they should be able to work in well-made facilities that aid, rather than impede, their mission.

Moreover, any facility that serves the homeless is located *somewhere,* and its immediate neighbors and the surrounding community deserve well-designed buildings that fit into the neighborhood, that help residents integrate themselves into the community, and that alleviate the concerns of local residents that the facility and its clients will compromise their own quality of life.

Much has been written over the past twenty years about homelessness—from social science, social welfare, demographic, economic, and public policy perspectives. Several recent books have described the enormous personal tragedies the homeless, particularly homeless children, suffer. All the analyses, studies, and life stories point to one inescapable truth: to help people get off the streets, regain control of their lives, and move into permanent housing, we need to design a variety of buildings that provide shelter, transitional housing, and support services. Once we accept this proposition, we should strive to make these buildings as good as we can. The architecture of creating buildings for the homeless is the focus of this book.

In preparation for writing this book, I interviewed directors of nonprofit service providers, public officials, architects, and many homeless and formerly homeless individuals. These interviews took place in Los Angeles, San Diego, the Bay Area, and New York City. I also conducted interviews on the phone and through e-mail with people across the country. But California, particularly the Bay Area, figures prominently in this book. It is the place I know best, having spent my entire professional life in the state. California, with its golden promises, benign climate, and social diversity, attracts people from all over the country and all over the world. Between 1980 and 2000, the state's population increased by about 40 percent, from 23.7 million in 1980, to 29.8 million in 1990, to 33.9 million in 2000.[1] As a result, California has a desperate shortage of housing, especially affordable housing, and a large and growing homeless population. Over the years, many counties and cities in California have tried various approaches to housing the homeless, from informal encampments constructed by the homeless (and tolerated, if not formally approved, by municipalities) to multimillion-dollar, state-of-the-art shelters. I discuss many of these experiments in this book, but the problems and solutions that I examine apply equally to large cities, small towns, suburbs, and rural areas across the United States.

The buildings that we construct are a reflection of our values and our culture. At its best, architecture not only reflects but also serves society; it has a duty to provide for those with the greatest need and the fewest options. Thus architecture should do more than provide homeless people with shelter: it must sustain their hope and their dignity. This book is intended to help architects, public policymakers, and housing activists realize that goal. I hope, too, that this book will enable communities to understand why the homeless need special facilities and to set aside their fears about the siting of these facilities in their neighborhoods.

ACKNOWLEDGMENTS

LIKE ARCHITECTURE, writing a book is a collaborative effort. I have relied on many people, and they have responded generously at various stages of this work, from the initial research to the final production.

Many individuals took time to sit for interviews during the book's early stages. Muzzy Rosenblatt was particularly helpful in arranging meetings and tours in New York City. Matt Stokes and Elizabeth Byrne assisted in the literature research. Amy Einsohn, Charles Dibble, and Sue Heinemann provided editorial and conceptual advice. My wife, Joanne Cuthbertson, herself both an author and editor, provided ongoing support and insightful advice. She also accompanied me to many homeless facilities and worked beside me serving holiday meals at some of these. Many people reviewed the manuscript at various stages and provided valuable counsel and input. Among them, I particularly want to thank Michael Underhill, Barbara Solomon, and Robert Gutman.

Jim Clark, director emeritus of the University of California Press, once again provided the initial support and motivation to put in writing what I had been doing and thinking about for several years.

My colleagues at Davis & Joyce architects—Lisa Joyce, Kevin Kodama, and Carolyn Greis—worked with me on all the projects of the firm discussed in the book. Many other architects and their clients provided materials and information and gave me access to their facilities.

I was also provided with financial support from College of Letters and Sciences, Humanities Research Fellowship of the University of California at Berkeley, and the John Simon Guggenheim Foundation.

Finally I want to thank my clients and those they serve. They are the inspiration.

INTRODUCTION

WHAT IS POSSIBLE and desirable when designing a new facility for the homeless? What should it look like, and what kind of feeling should it convey? Should it call attention to itself or maintain a low profile? Should it resemble a conventional house or be more like a dormitory? What type of spaces should be included? Given budgetary constraints, what is the proper balance between function, quality of construction, and architectural delight? Those who serve the homeless, and especially the architects who design facilities that accommodate the homeless, must confront these questions.

This book examines how architects have approached the challenge of designing facilities for the homeless. Some responses are modest and discreet; others are more assertive. I have chosen to begin with what might be the most complex and comprehensive facility for the homeless yet built: the Joan Kroc Center at the St. Vincent de Paul Village in San Diego. It both indicates what is possible and introduces many of the issues addressed in the chapters that follow.

The 110,000-square-foot Joan Kroc Center opened in the summer of 1987 at a cost of $11.6 million (equivalent to approximately $20 million today). The building is largely the work of Father Joe Carroll, known as "Father Joe," who raised most of the money privately, inspiring donors with his vision and force of personality. Not long after its completion, the center became known as the Taj Mahal of shelters.[1] It can accommodate 350 people and serve more than 1,300 meals a day. The comprehensiveness of the center's programs, the range of populations that the center serves, and the grandness of its architecture have drawn national attention, including reports about the center and Father Joe himself on CBS's *60 Minutes* and ABC's *Nightline*.

The building, designed by Fred A. De Santo and the firm of Krommenhock, McKeown & Associates (now KMA Architecture and Engineering), is in the Spanish mission style, common in Southern California (figure 1). When first built in the American West, the missions were safe-havens, placed a day's travel apart; their courtyards offered protection, much like a wagon circle. The use of this model in the Joan Kroc Center has symbolic significance that transcends its associations with regional architecture. The cross prominently displayed on the center's bell tower, the chapel, and the cloistered courtyard conveys a clear message that the services offered by the center to the homeless are grounded in the Christian faith. This is a sanctuary, a protected place for the most vulnerable, in which they will receive sustenance, shelter, and renewed spirit.

Underlying these religious associations, how-

FIGURE 1 The Joan Kroc Center at the St. Vincent de Paul Village, San Diego. The center's form, reminiscent of California's Spanish-style missions, defines its function as a safe haven for the homeless.

ever, is a smoothly operating complex. The bell towers, for example, have a practical function: they are part of an energy-efficient ventilating system that takes advantage of prevailing breezes, reducing the need for air conditioning and lowering operational costs. A garage beneath the building is a convenience for the professionals—doctors, social workers, and psychologists—who volunteer at the center. As Father Joe has noted, "What volunteer doctor will want to park his Mercedes on these streets at night?"[2] The dining room converts into a basketball court (figure 2). The facility is monitored by dozens of security cameras, and the mechanical system is computer-operated in order

FIGURE 2 The large dining hall at the Joan Kroc Center can be converted to a basketball court.

to maximize its efficiency. To avoid the expense of replacing lost keys, bedrooms are fitted with electronic locks. Children have access to a day care center and an elementary school that is part of the San Diego school district.

The focus of all these functions is the large courtyard (figure 3). Most of the common rooms—classrooms, the dining room, the workshop, and chapel—either have views into or are accessed from this space. A loggia borders the courtyard at ground level, mitigating the scale of the three-story building that defines the space (figure 4). Following the tradition of mission-style architecture, it provides views into an open, public space, facilitates circulation around the courtyard, and protects residents from sun and occasional rain. Initially the courtyard, intended as a place for contemplation, was empty of trees, benches, flower beds, or art; its features were limited to a fountain and a pathway that bisected the large expanse of lawn. Over the years, the grass has given way to Astroturf (a better play surface for children), and half the courtyard is filled with play equipment.

FIGURE 3 The walled courtyard of the Joan Kroc Center, protected from its urban context, is used as a playground.

The visual vocabulary of the California missions imbues the design of the center with a spiritual feeling, and the monastic associations are underscored by the deep-set windows, arched openings, beamed ceilings, and cloistered courtyard. Father Joe views these architectural elements as signatures of the entire enterprise, sending a message to the residents that this is a dignified and important place, and that by association, so are they.[3] It sends a similar message to the community and to those who donate the $20 million each year it takes to operate the complex.

Father Joe believes that good architecture is critical to helping the homeless, even though it requires more money. His architects often suggested ways to reduce costs, but he argued that these cost savings would be counterproductive. Father Joe's involvement in the design of the center extended even to the smallest elements of the building, such as window blinds housed between double panes of glass that never need cleaning or repair. For him, such details and embellishments are integral to the success of the building and the programs within.

Within weeks of its completion, the Joan Kroc Center, designed primarily for homeless families with children, proved too small to meet the demand

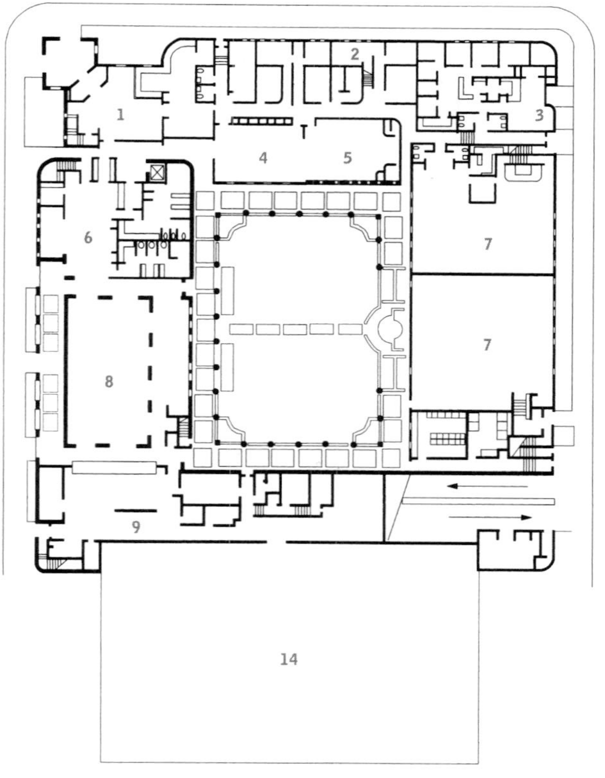

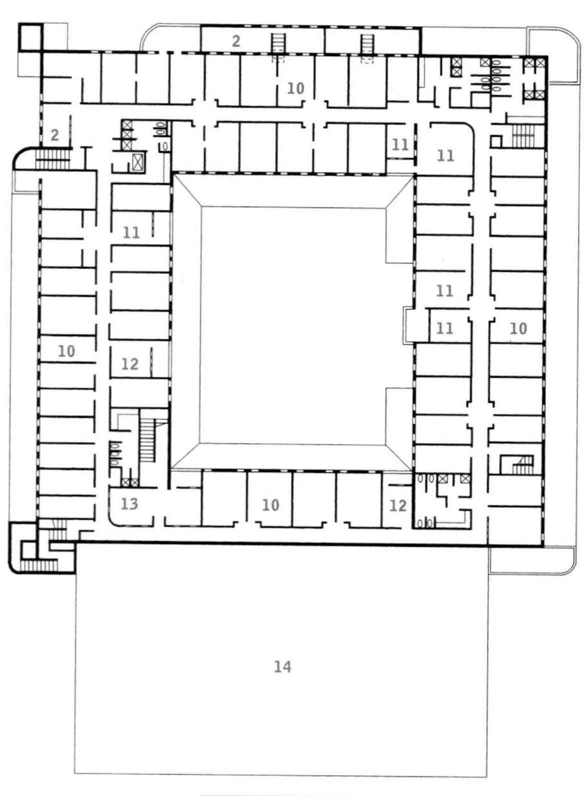

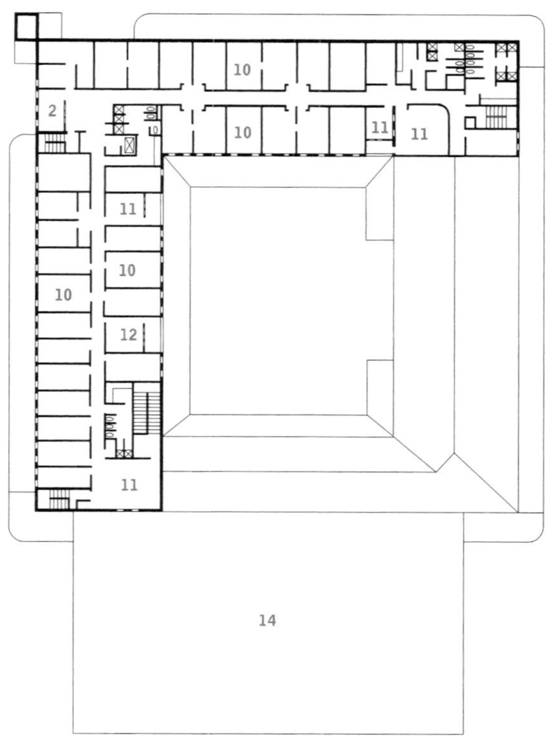

FIGURE 4 The plans of the Joan Kroc Center.

KEY	
1 Entry	8 Dining
2 Offices	9 Kitchen
3 Clinic	10 Bedrooms
4 Multi-use	11 TV room/lounge
5 Chapel	12 Library
6 Day room	13 Resource center
7 Classroom	14 Existing structure

FIGURE 5 The St. Vincent de Paul Village comprises renovated buildings and new construction, as well as the surrounding streets.

for its services. Program consultants had told Father Joe that the clinic he planned was too large, and they expressed doubt that doctors would volunteer their time, but the clinic in fact was too small, both for the number of clients and for the number of physicians who volunteered to staff it. In a new and larger clinic housed in a separate building, the University of California at San Diego Medical School plays a prominent role, to such an extent that some doctors spend their entire residency there. This new facility includes a large dental office whose walls are adorned with before-and-after pictures of homeless patients with new dental work and broad smiles.

In the years since the completion of the Joan Kroc Center, Father Joe has added several buildings to the complex, now known as the St. Vincent de Paul Village (figure 5). These include a converted warehouse that is physically connected to the Joan Kroc Center, a new building constructed across the street in 1993, and most recently a midrise apartment building containing studio units. The additions reflect an expansion of the programs sponsored by the organization, including new housing for single men and women. None of these buildings is as distinctive as the cornerstone center, but all share similar architectural features, such as arched windows, a courtyard, or balconies, which unify the space.

While Father Joe sometimes describes St. Vincent's as a campus, one that includes his own residence in a historic Victorian house across the street from the Joan Kroc Center, he prefers the notion of a village. A campus is associated with younger people, but a village is a city made small, and the people that reside within are therefore citizens of a vibrant, diverse place. Everything they need—a restaurant, housing, recreation, and services—is there. The village even has its own newspaper. The one missing element that has yet to be realized is a commercial enterprise that would generate income and provide a means for residents to develop skills through job training.

Critics have faulted several aspects of the St. Vincent de Paul Village. The facility's size, extending over several city blocks, has raised concerns among local politicians that the village has simply drawn in the homeless from other parts of the city, or those who are living with friends or family and therefore at a slight remove from homelessness, and concentrated them within the facility without reducing homelessness (the syndrome of "if you build it, they will come"). Certainly, it could be argued that the size and the complexity of the St. Vincent de Paul Village have created a corral for the homeless. But Father Joe maintains that you can treat the entire person only if you have all the needed personnel and facilities, and that the range of services that the village provides would not be feasible without a large population. More important, because the organization relies primarily on donations and not public funding, it can control all the elements of its operations. (With government funds come restrictions on sharing information about clients and patients. Those who undertake the program must consent to the sharing of their personal information among the programs and services.) This provides flexibility, with little bureaucratic interference, in whatever treatment, intervention, or training is deemed appropriate.

What the homeless give up in privacy and personal freedom at the St. Vincent de Paul Village is compensated by a high level of services and security. Security is a defining element of the village. In addition to the electronic systems, German shepherds patrol the grounds; individuals posing as homeless clients regularly test the quality of the programs. To some critics, such a system smacks of Big Brother, and for the homeless who distrust authority or who have been in other highly structured institutions, such as prisons, the village is a hard sell. But for others (particularly women and children, who are most vulnerable on the streets) these security measures are welcome. Father Joe equates this management style with that of Las Vegas resorts: to prevent you from going elsewhere, they provide you with everything you might need in a safe setting.

The village has grown as neighboring sites and buildings became available for purchase and as funds were raised for construction and staffing. Each added element is accompanied by an open space that has become part of the surrounding city. The street that separates the Joan Kroc Center from the newest building is fast becoming a public plaza for the complex. The street is closed to traffic, and there are plans to landscape the space. The mid-rise apartment building is across yet another street.

Father Joe was warned that this village for the homeless would not be feasible. Naysayers predicted crime and graffiti, but no one has seen graffiti within the village, and there is no crime, with the exception of occasional fights in the cafeteria line. For Father Joe the issue was not one of feasibility but rather of carrying out the village's mission well. His message, and that of the village, is "Don't settle for less than the best."[4] He has put his considerable persuasive powers behind this belief, sometimes making curious and expensive gestures that seem to have little to do with the basic mission but much to do with this overall vision. One side of the mid-rise building is decorated with a $1 million mural, the largest mosaic in the country.

How successful is this approach? Father Joe claims that 80 percent of those who undergo the entire program move on to permanent housing and an independent life. Furthermore, the village is full. But most telling is that when a mother and her children arrive and see the hustle and bustle of the lobby—a clean and appealing place—rather than ask, "Do we *have* to stay here?" they ask, "*Can* we stay here?"

The St. Vincent de Paul Village is one example of what is possible given the commitment of an organization and the strong vision of an individual. It accommodates a range of housing for the homeless that constitutes what is known as "the continuum of care" (table 1). This principle acknowledges that although the homeless need emergency shelter, they also need access to stable and secure places in which to live that provide the services required to enable them to be independent. These elements of the continuum of care are the focus of this book.

TABLE—THE HOUSING CONTINUUM

Housing type in the United States varies depending on one's ability to pay.
At one end is the homeless shelter, at the other is the owner-occupied house.
Regardless of the type or the occupant's ability to pay, all forms of housing include some subsidy.
The focus of this book is the portion of this housing for those least able to pay.
This is known as the *Continuum of Care.*

Form of housing	Characteristics	Residents / form of subsidy
Emergency Shelter	Generally organized in dormitory-style wards, most present-day shelters also have on-site social services and case-management programs. Separate shelters, or portions of shelters, house different homeless populations such as single adults, families (most often with a single parent), seniors, and young adults. The duration of occupancy varies, but is generally weeks or months.	Those without the ability to pay for housing. Many have physical and mental health problems. *A combination of public funds and private donations.*
Transitional Shelter	These often include a combination of living arrangements, from dormitory-style wards to rooms housing six to eight people each. Programs emphasize social services, the development of life skills, and job training. Residents undertake programs at the facility intended to help them become independent. Separate shelters, or portions of shelters, house specific homeless populations such as single adults, families (most often with a single parent), seniors, and young adults. The duration of occupancy varies, generally six months, but it may be as long as a year or two.	Those without the ability to pay for housing. Many have physical and mental health problems. *A combination of public funds and private donations.*
Transitional Housing	Transitional housing may take a number of different forms including single room occupancy (SRO) buildings with small independent studio units. Boardinghouses and other shared residences are also common. Social services are included, but not always	Those with some ability to pay for housing, often through disability payments or other rent subsidy. Many have physical and mental health problems.

(continued)

Form of housing	Characteristics	Residents / form of subsidy
Transitional Housing (continued)	on-site. The duration of occupancy varies, but may be as long as a year or two. The lack of sufficient permanent housing has led to long-term occupancy of transitional housing.	*A combination of public funds and private donations.*
Supportive Housing	The first element of the continuum to be treated as permanent housing. Many features are comparable to transitional housing. Supportive housing may take a number of different forms, including SROs, but other multi-unit buildings with larger apartments and even single-family houses can be supportive housing. Social services and specific programs for residents are integral to the housing, although they are not always provided on-site.	Those with some ability to pay for housing, often through disability payments or other rent subsidy. Many have physical and mental health problems. *A combination of public funds and private donations.*
Public Housing	Public housing is created specifically for those with insufficient income to afford the market rent. Funding programs vary. Some are aimed at those with very low incomes, others at those at an income level of less than 50 percent of the area's median income. Public housing, most often in multi-family apartment buildings, is designed for specific groups such as families or seniors. Originally developed primarily by the federal government, this housing is now supported by nonprofit community development corporations, most often in low-rise buildings. The federal government finances the renovation of older public housing projects.	Those with some ability to pay for housing who are expected to spend 30 percent of their income on rent. *A combination of public funds and private donations. Many projects are financed through tax credits allocated by state and federal government.*
Assisted Housing	This is privately developed market-rate housing that also accommodates individuals or families who qualify for rental subsidies (housing vouchers). The housing is not specifically created or designed for a low-income population and takes various forms, from apartment complexes to single-family houses.	Those with some ability to pay who are expected to spend 30 percent of their income on rent. *Federal Section 8 vouchers make up the difference between the market rent and that 30 percent.*

Form of housing	Characteristics	Residents / form of subsidy
Rental Housing	Rental housing is privately developed and most often takes the form of apartments or attached dwellings. It includes any housing that is not owned by the occupant.	Those who can pay the market rate and either choose to rent or cannot afford to buy. *Some states, such as California, offer renters' credits, a modest form of subsidy.*
Owner-Occupied		
First-Time Buyer	The house type can be a single-family house of any size or it may be in a multifamily building. Sixty-eight percent of Americans own their own dwelling.	Those who can pay market rates. *Tax deductions for mortgage interest and real estate tax.*
Assisted Living and Congregate Care for Seniors	This housing is defined as specialized facilities that may include private or double-occupancy rooms. It generally includes group dining facilities, planned activities, social services, and health care.	Those who can pay the market rate, although some residents may be subsidized.

1 WHOSE PROBLEM IS IT?

HOMELESSNESS in the United States will not disappear anytime soon. The shortage of affordable housing, the widening gap between the minimum wage and a living wage (defined as the income needed to support one adult and one child at a very modest standard of living), the nation's growing population, the gentrification of downtowns, the longer life span of the chronically ill made possible by advances in medical science, the dwindling number of community mental health facilities, weakening family ties, the ongoing drug epidemic—all these trends make it certain that homelessness will be with us for the foreseeable future.

We therefore need to find effective ways to help the homeless move off the streets and regain control of their lives. For most homeless people, the need for basic shelter—a dry, warm, safe place with a bed—is acute and immediate. The design of that shelter matters: to the homeless, to those who work with them, to the neighboring community, and to society at large. And although building emergency short-stay shelters is a crucial first step, we also need to create transitional housing for those who can be expected to return to the market economy, and permanent housing with support services for those who cannot.

Architecture is not the first thing that most people think of when they consider how best to help the homeless. But architecture can play an important role in creating facilities that sustain the dignity of people who have fallen on hard times. Well-designed facilities can also encourage the reluctant (often called the "shelter-resistant") to seek services by reassuring them that they are not about to enter a prisonlike fortress, a depressing warehouse for discarded people, or a dangerous madhouse.

WHO ARE THE HOMELESS?

It is impossible to know exactly how many people in the United States are homeless: How do you count them? When do you count? Whom do you count? The numbers differ if you count on a mild spring day or on a raw day during winter. Do you count only those in shelters, jails, and hospitals or include those on the street? The method and timing of counting can lead to two different types of numbers. The point-in-time method identifies the number on a specific day. But homelessness is often not a permanent situation; people go in and out of homelessness or may escape it altogether after only a brief period. Another method, known as the period prevalence count, attempts to provide a more accurate picture by identifying the number of homeless over a longer period.[1] Best estimates place the number of homeless people in the United States on any given night at above 700,000. The number of people who experience a period of homelessness sometime during the calendar year may well be over 2 million.[2] This figure, it is worth noting, excludes people who are technically not "homeless" but live in overcrowded, unhealthy, or unsafe conditions—for example, a family of five in a 10-by-10-foot room in San Francisco's Chinatown, sharing a single kitchen and four toilets with sixty other people.[3]

Given the difficulties of calculating the number of homeless people, demographic analyses of the homeless population are based on estimates and guesswork.[4] The demographics that most confound public perceptions are these:

- The fastest-growing segment of the homeless population consists of single parents, usually young women, and their children. In the early 1990s families comprised a small percentage of the homeless, but in many parts of the country today 40 percent of the homeless are families.[5]
- About 22 percent of the homeless are employed.[6] Some are earning minimum wage, but others earn quite a bit more. Standard guidelines recommend that no more than 30 percent of income be allocated to housing; the median rents in certain cities would thus require a wage of approximately $20 per hour. In San Francisco, one of the nation's most expensive cities for housing, an annual household income of $80,000 is needed to afford the rental on an average two-bedroom apartment under the 30 percent guidelines.[7]
- Less than 10 percent of the homeless are older than 55, but the number of homeless seniors is increasing. Because most of them are on fixed incomes, they cannot afford market-rate housing. Some have no income, many are in poor health, and many are women.[8]
- The chronically homeless, those that we most often see on the streets, constitute between 10 and 25 percent of the homeless.[9]
- Military veterans constitute about 23 percent of the homeless, about the same percentage as in the general population.[10]

Other statistics confirm public perceptions of the homeless, although the percentage of homeless people suffering from mental illness and substance abuse is lower than one might expect:

- About 30 percent of the homeless have some form of mental illness, including depression.[11] Among them are the most "shelter-resistant": individuals who distrust authority, cannot abide by rules, and feel threatened by group living.

- About 30 percent of the homeless are substance abusers.[12] For some, alcohol and drugs contributed to their homelessness; for others, the despair of homelessness led to the alcohol and drug abuse.

- About 10 percent of the homeless live in rural areas.[13] Every community—even wealthy enclaves like Beverly Hills and the Hamptons—has homeless people.

As these statistics suggest, the old face of homelessness may have been that of a grizzled middle-aged alcoholic male who just wanted to be left alone. The new picture of homelessness is far more diverse. It includes women in their twenties and thirties—sometimes employed—and their children. These families want assistance, although parents, especially women who have been sexually or physically abused, may be reluctant to enter shelters that they perceive as dangerous or dirty. The new picture also includes men and women of all ages who have complex medical problems: HIV or AIDS, physical disabilities, and mental illness exacerbated by substance abuse. In the short term all these people need shelter, but they need much more than shelter if they are to succeed in getting off and staying off the streets. They may need substance abuse treatment, medical treatment, nursing care, psychiatric care or psychological counseling, financial counseling, job training, day care, education for their children—the list of their needs is long.

HOW DID THEY BECOME HOMELESS?

People become homeless when three things happen to them: they lose their residence, they are unable to find a new one, and they cannot convince anyone to take them in. A quick survey of the life events that may trigger this sequence suggests that only some of the responsibility for homelessness rests with the individual: socioeconomic trends play a decisive role, as do simple events of everyday life. For example, people may lose their residence when:

their household disintegrates (the newly divorced, widowed, or orphaned; teenagers or adult children evicted by their parents; roommates evicted by other roommates; doubled-up families evicted by relatives or friends);

they flee their homes (runaway teens, battered spouses);

they are released from a residential institution—a hospital or prison—or leave the armed services;

they lose a live-in job as a health-care aide, groundskeeper, or on-site counselor;

a natural disaster (fire, flood, or earthquake) makes their home uninhabitable;

they are unable to pay their mortgage and their home is foreclosed;

they are evicted for failing to pay the rent;

they are evicted for nonfinancial reasons: the landlord empties the building in preparation for selling it; an apartment is converted into a condominium; the building is condemned by the city or seized through eminent domain for another purpose.

The inability to find a new residence is often a matter of economics: people cannot find housing within their budget or close enough to their job;

they do not have enough savings to put down a deposit on a new apartment; prospective landlords reject their applications because they have bad credit or are unemployed. Sometimes homelessness is a matter of competency: the individual does not have the skills or the fortitude to search for inexpensive housing. Alcohol and drugs may play a part, but illiteracy or an emotional or physical disability may also make it difficult to read newspaper advertisments, make phone calls, visit available apartments, fill out applications, or make a good impression during an interview with the landlord.

Not every person who is unable to find new housing ends up homeless. Many rely on family and friends to take them in or lend them enough money to tide them over. Those who become homeless are those who have no friends or family willing or able to house them—either because their own situation is precarious or because the newly evicted are too needy (suffering from medical or psychiatric problems, for example) to fit in their households.

At the top of the list of recent socioeconomic trends that cause or exacerbate homelessness is the nationwide housing shortage, especially the dire shortage of affordable housing. California, for example, produced 110,000 housing units each year during the 1990s, but twice that number were needed to meet demand, and by the end of the decade the deficit exceeded 1 million units.[14] But even if the market could supply the necessary number of new housing units, it is unlikely that all those units would be in the right places, at the right prices, and with the features needed most by the frail elderly, the physically disabled, and other at-risk populations. The builder of last resort used to be the federal government, but in the early 1970s it began to abandon this role, and by the end of the 1980s federal funding for housing had fallen by 72 percent.[15]

Even as we fail to build enough new units to meet demand, we are losing affordable units to urban renewal. San Francisco, for example, lost over 6,000 single-room occupancy hotel (SRO) units between 1975 and 1980,[16] and the Loma Prieta earthquake in 1989 rendered hundreds of the remaining SROs uninhabitable. Other cities had similar losses as urban renewal and conversion to other uses eliminated what civic leaders considered marginal or substandard housing.

The loss of SROs hints at another trend in housing that hurts the poor. Most Americans have benefited from our evolving notion of what constitutes decent housing: today we expect more square footage, better ventilation, fire detection and sprinkler systems—far more than what our grandparents' generation required. But as the perceptions of habitability continue to change, and as municipal codes are rewritten to stricter standards, the cost of building even the most modest housing increases. No one wants to resurrect the six-floor walk-up tenement, but the expectation that every studio apartment will have its own kitchen and bathroom greatly increases the cost per unit.

Changes in the housing market have been the most immediate cause of homelessness; changes in the labor market are a close second. Two hundred years ago, unskilled workers were thrown out of work by the Industrial Revolution; the technological revolution of the last several decades has created an entire new class of unskilled workers. Jobs for unskilled workers do not pay enough to cover the cost of housing in most cities. Over the past decade, the nation has lost 1.4 million well-paying jobs in manufacturing, and the minimum wage has increased by only $1.35 per hour.[17] By 2002 more than 11 percent of Americans were living in poverty, and those with the lowest incomes were the most likely not to have medical insurance.[18]

The shift from employer-sponsored defined-benefit pension plans to worker-financed 401(k) plans has reduced the income security of retired workers.

Another social policy that continues to play a role in creating homelessness is the deinstitutionalization of the mentally ill, which began in the 1960s. The goal of the policy was to enable mentally ill people to live in the least restrictive environment they could manage. Those who did not require constant care and who posed no threat to themselves or others were to live in the community, with access to comprehensive community mental health services, including halfway houses and group homes. Those facilities, however, were never built in sufficient numbers. During the initial wave of deinstitutionalization, the population of the nation's public psychiatric hospitals fell sharply (from 500,000 in the 1950s to 100,000 by the 1970s).[19] Now, some thirty years later, the population of federal, state, and county mental health facilities is below 100,000 while the country's population has increased, along with the numbers of those needing mental health care.[20] Mentally ill people who do not have families to support them, either at home or in a private institution, and cannot hold a job are at great risk of becoming homeless; homelessness, it is safe to say, further destabilizes them. They are also likely to end up in jail for disorderly conduct, belligerent panhandling, or creating "a public nuisance." Concurrent with deinstitutionalization, efforts to protect the rights of the mentally ill made it difficult to institutionalize people without their consent. In the absence of institutional care, these individuals, lacking the support of family and unable to find or hold jobs, are rendered homeless.

In the mid-twentieth century the great majority of the homeless were middle-aged. That median age is now the low to mid-thirties.[21] Some attribute this change to the use of crack cocaine. It may take several decades for alcohol to render an individual homeless; often it is only in middle age that the disease has taken its toll, with the loss of family, employment, and money. The damage that alcohol does to a person over a few decades, crack cocaine can do in a few years. The easy availability and low cost of the drug hasten the syndrome.

Finally, during the 1990s most states in the nation enacted "get tough on crime" laws that sent more people to prison and imposed longer sentences. Released prisoners are especially vulnerable to homelessness: the longer the prison term, the weaker the individual's ties to family and friends and the harder it is to find a job. Released prisoners generally have the greatest resistance to entering the shelter system, which they perceive as another form of incarceration.

THE SOCIAL CONTRACT

The ubiquity of street homeless, made more visible by the extensive coverage of homelessness by the news media, might suggest to some that this a relatively new phenomenon in the United States. It is not. Soldiers returning to urban areas from the Civil War were often homeless. Thousands were made homeless during the Great Depression; many lost their homes in other economic downturns and recessions. But during the latter half of the nineteenth century and the first half of the twentieth, the homeless were primarily middle-aged men isolated in the skid rows of our cities; they were not seen as a daily affront to the general population or a widespread social problem for the simple reason that they were often not seen. They worked intermittently as day laborers at the many jobs available as America urbanized.

Fifty years ago, the general population did not view homelessness as a scourge, but as the consequence of a mobile society. Individuals without roots or permanent dwellings were often romanticized in the mid-twentieth century. To travel on the open road, ride the rails, and seek adventure were seen as wanderlust. Personal mobility, especially a mobile workforce, enabled this country to expand. Trailer parks dotted the roadsides, and though some disparaged their inhabitants, the parks had much the same appeal as today's recreational vehicle parks. We called these homeless men itinerant workers, hoboes, or even knights of the road.[22] Depression-era movies such as *My Man Godfrey* (1936) depicted the homeless sympathetically—as forgotten men, perhaps, but nonetheless salvageable—and the comic message has continued to inform such recent films as *Down and Out in Beverly Hills* (1986). One of comedian Red Skelton's best-known characters, Freddie the Freeloader, was a tragic but sympathetic soul. Now we have street people, panhandlers, bag ladies, or worse. But despite the nation's tendency to ignore or discount homelessness as a major (and growing) social problem, it clearly existed, and the roots of today's problem had taken hold. A homeless person, it was thought, was responsible for his plight. He was wayward, not a victim of circumstances. This attitude persists, although it is increasingly clear that homelessness is rarely a choice.

This is particularly true for homeless children, who are the most tragically affected and incur the greatest long-term costs. They are vulnerable to drugs and alcohol, and their overall situation, particularly the risk of malnutrition, makes them more prone to illness than housed children. They have not received the vaccinations that require regular visits to a doctor over a period of time. Their schooling—if they even go to school—suffers because poor health and lack of sleep make it difficult for them to pay attention in the classroom. Communicable diseases spread easily in open-ward shelters. Exposure to the elements aggravates respiratory ailments, especially among the very young (asthma is common among homeless children). Unstable housing limits the social network of these children, who then become susceptible to other behavioral problems.

> I had a lot of friends at my old school, but now I'm in a school where nobody knows me. I'm always left out because I'm new here. One girl asked me where I lived, but I didn't tell her. I got scared 'cause she'd think we're homeless and that Mom's lazy or doesn't take care of us. But that's not true. My Mom wants to work again. She's trying hard to get another job.[23]

> My name is Wayne. Mom and I got here last night. I sure hope we get to stay for a while because this is better than where we were before. I don't think we will. They won't let you do drugs here, and Mom uses.[24]

Among adults, homelessness exacerbates existing health problems, but poor nutrition and exposure to the elements pose particular risks to the elderly, as they do to children. Existing substance abuse problems are likely to grow worse among the subculture of the homeless, in which drugs and alcohol are used to soothe the symptoms of depression. Small medical problems become acute, since many homeless people will not seek medical care until their condition is critical and they require hospitalization. The homeless are often victims, as well as perpetrators, of crime, particularly crimes related to drugs. All these conditions place a burden on local police, jails, courts, and hospitals.

The homeless have no phone, no mail, no place to receive visitors. The loss of the means of social contact exacerbates their feelings of isolation. Some homeless people report that they find themselves staring at people's keys, a poignant reminder of the extent of their own loss, since they no longer have the things that require keys: a home, a car, and an office.

Now that homelessness is so widespread and acute, each of us must decide how much we can and should do. What is our responsibility to those caught in this tragic circumstance? Might our actions (or inactions) be making the problem worse? For example, community resistance to an affordable housing project (or demands that its size be decreased) has an impact on homelessness, driving up the cost of housing and reducing access to it. We confront a moral dilemma whenever we encounter a homeless person asking for money. Will they use the money for food, shelter, or medicine, or for drugs or alcohol? We make a judgment about whether a handout will perpetuate a homeless person's situation, lessen that person's suffering for the short term, or provide real assistance.

We make the same judgment, on a larger scale, when we build shelters or other emergency facilities for the homeless. In providing these, do we create a permanent underclass? Wouldn't jobs and a living wage be a better way to provide access to housing? Further, the more we increase emergency aid, particularly shelters, the more homeless we have. Those who might have resided with friends or family now have an alternative. With so many in need, the shelter population increases with the supply. Some shelter operators suggest that shelters may discourage people from escaping homelessness by reinforcing dependency and undermining initiative.

Architecture plays a part in this dilemma. Once we decide to create shelters for the homeless, we strive to make them safe, clean, and friendly places where the homeless will want to go. The more we do so, the more people want to use them and to stay. But if we do not build appropriate and decent places, we simply reinforce the stereotypes and perpetuate the problem. Many believe that housing is the government's responsibility. After all, we provide billions of dollars in aid for those in need throughout the world: why shouldn't we be willing to do the same for those who struggle in this country?

The federal government's view was that homelessness was an emergency, like a flood or earthquake; monies were therefore managed by the Federal Emergency Management Agency (FEMA). In 1983, the Federal Interagency Task Force on Food and Shelter for the Homeless began allocating functions to be administered locally throughout the United States. In a 1979 New York class action suit *(Callahan v. Carey),* homeless advocates won a ruling from the state supreme court that required accommodation for every homeless person seeking shelter. The Stewart B. McKinney Homeless Assistance Act, signed into law in 1987, established an annual federal allocation of funds for the homeless administered by the Department of Housing and Urban Development (HUD), an acknowledgment that homelessness had become a chronic problem, not an emergency. HUD's programs targeted specific aspects of the homeless problem and specific populations within the homeless community; the HOPWA program (Housing Opportunities for Persons with AIDS), for example, granted funding to people with AIDS. By 2002 HUD funding for the homeless had grown to $1.1 billion in a total federal budget of nearly $2 trillion.[25] Such grants, as well as aid from the Department of Health and Human Services for health, education, and support services for battered women and teens, suggest the range of issues that homeless people confront. More than 40,000 programs nationwide provide assistance to the homeless.[26] While many are funded by the government, most depend equally on private support. But even here, unity of purpose is no guarantee against conflicts.

A group in New Jersey, for example, brings food into Manhattan for the homeless, but some who provide services to the city's homeless told me that they see this as interfering with their own mission to get people off the streets and into shelters where other services are provided.

Public works departments, police, health departments, and service providers all ascribe a dollar figure to their work on homelessness. Perhaps the greatest—and most incalculable—costs, however, are the deleterious effects on society when a large and growing segment of the population is in such dire need.

WHAT ARCHITECTURE CAN DO

Some architects maintain that best way to achieve affordable housing is to recognize cost limitations at the outset and make compromises on space standards, amenities, and even quality; others argue, as I have, that affordable housing should be indistinguishable from nearby housing so that the residents will not be stigmatized and will feel a part of the surrounding community. When it comes to housing for the homeless, however, the crisis is so pressing that I have come to accept the notion that we must compromise on some standards in designing certain types of facilities for the homeless. These compromises, in turn, require more involvement—not less—by architects, who can apply standards of good design to make small spaces functional and dignified, and manage modest budgets to create safe and welcoming places. Because so many homeless people have lived in institutions at some time in their lives, they naturally distrust shelters, which they see as yet another institution. If the design of a facility can help the homeless feel that they have found a safe haven, they are more likely to come in and ask for help.

Architects can also play a critical role in overcoming communities' reluctance to have homeless facilities built in their midst. If shelters and transitional housing are to succeed, they must be situated in residential and commercial areas, near public transportation, jobs, social services, and schools—not at the outskirts of town or at the margins of industrial zones. In recent years, some homeless facilities have been placed on decommissioned military bases. The price is right (the land and some buildings are free), and many policymakers feel that removing the homeless from the temptations of the streets gives them a better chance of focusing on job training and other life skills. Nevertheless, the consensus among those who work with the homeless is that the more remote the facility, the less effective it is likely to be. The homeless generally do not have cars, and many do not or cannot drive. The farther they have to travel to obtain services, search for permanent housing, or visit friends and family, the harder their lives will be. Placing shelters and transitional housing out of the way may please homeowners and business owners, but it is a shortsighted public policy.

Architects can also help policymakers and the general public understand a key economic fact: it costs more to care for a homeless family in a shelter than in permanent housing. In New York City, for example, it costs $3,000 per month to shelter a homeless family, but only $742 per month to subsidize an apartment and provide supportive services.[27] Recent studies have shown that building permanent supportive housing for mentally ill homeless people pays for itself through the reduction in services.[28] Creating buildings does entails costs, as we will see in chapter 3, but it is clear that thoughtful architecture is a major part of the solution.

Perhaps the architect's most important challenge when designing for the homeless is to restore a sense of dignity to the residents. This should be the first objective, whether the facility is a temporary emergency shelter, a transitional shelter, or an SRO. A homeless person is an isolated person. A place that makes people feel welcome, comfortable, and safe signals that someone cares about them and that they are worthy of this concern. Choice and self-determination are cornerstones of dignity, and a homeless person has few options. An architect can create a diversity of spaces even in a single building to give people choices.

THE ARCHITECT AND HOMELESSNESS 2

ARCHITECTURE REFLECTS social attitudes, aspirations, and values. The design of churches and government buildings, for example, is often intended to inspire awe and command respect; mansions and corporate headquarters communicate social status or power. Much of our history with respect to housing, however, has been dominated by an attitude that those at the lower end of the economic scale deserve little, and certainly not pleasant or well-designed buildings. Designing for the disadvantaged was long viewed as an undertaking unsuited to architects, whose status was defined by that of their patrons.

By the 1960s, however, many architects began to see housing, particularly low-income housing, as a social and professional responsibility. Research on the social and cultural implications of housing design focused on how dwellings reflect identity, both to the individuals who inhabit them and to others: "For most people the self is a fragile and vulnerable entity; we wish therefore to envelop ourselves in a symbol-for-self which is familiar, solid, inviolate, unchanging."[1] Architects involved in housing design began to realize that good buildings can improve the quality of life, both physical and emotional. This principle is fundamental to the design of facilities for the homeless.

During the last hundred years, the options for the homeless with respect to accommodation included shelters, beds, or small private spaces within commercially operated hotels often known as flophouses, private rooms in residential hotels known as SROs (single-room occupancy hotels)—or the streets. None were "familiar, solid, inviolate, unchanging." Each of these choices survives in some form, but the recent participation of architects in thinking about how these choices can more sympathetically serve their constituencies has done much to improve the quality of accommodations for the homeless. Supportive housing—facilities designed expressly for homeless people that include a social service component—is a more recent and effective option.

This chapter is about how these forms of accommodation have evolved, and how that evolution reflects changes in attitudes among architects toward the homeless. Tracing the precedents for housing the homeless documents how hard it has been to make the leap from mere shelter to permanent, dignified housing. Architects have played a role in creating, perpetuating, and ultimately overcoming the persistent view of the homeless as outcasts to whom society's obligation (if any) stopped at rudimentary shelter.

THE HOUSING REFORMERS

An impetus toward social reform began to take hold within the architectural community as early as the 1860s. The deplorable living conditions and overcrowding associated with tenement housing led socially minded architects and housing reformers to call for building codes with provisions for basic sanitation and fire safety. Although well intended, these efforts had several unanticipated consequences. The enactment of New York City's first housing code in 1866 led to an increase in homelessness (a cause and effect that to some extent holds true to this day). First, the costs of constructing better and safer housing placed it out of the reach of the very poor. Second, housing reform was guided by assumptions among its advocates about which forms of housing constituted desirable accommodation. Kitchens and private bathrooms, for example, were deemed necessities, and many forms of housing that provided shelter at low cost, albeit with few amenities and little privacy, were seen as encouraging antisocial behavior and disappeared as a consequence. The single-family detached house remains an American ideal, a lingering result of this attitude and the government incentives (such as the deductibility of home mortgage payments and real estate taxes from taxable income) that reinforce it. Housing codes, regulations, gentrification, and zoning forced the extinction of SROs, boardinghouses, and lodging houses.[2] It is only now, a century later, that these options are being reconsidered as economically and socially viable forms of accommodation for the homeless.

At the beginning of the twentieth century, most viewed the homeless as a homogeneous group constituted of alcoholic middle-aged men. Social policy was informed by religion and sought to encourage these individuals to "see the error of their ways" and "pull themselves up by their bootstraps." The shelters took in derelicts—"drunks and vagrants"—but they also housed those who were simply out of work.[3] One group needed treatment, the other needed jobs. Institutional shelters often inflicted further damage on individuals who might have benefited from treatment, and they were unable to fulfill the needs of job-seekers, who were stigmatized both by residing in the shelters and by their association with the chronically homeless.

SHELTERS

THE EARLY SHELTERS

At its most basic level, architecture is about defining space to accommodate human activities—form *and* function. The architecture of the earliest shelters, in principle, should have reflected differences among the population that they served, but design counted for little in their construction, and the shelters themselves made no distinction among the populations they purported to serve. Facilities were spartan at best. The earliest shelters were set up as emergency facilities in the basements, hallways, and stairways of public buildings—often the local police station house (a reflection of the caretaker role of the police, not of real or imagined criminality among the homeless). People slept on chairs, stairs, and tabletops as well as on the floor, and these shelters sought principally to contain and control the homeless.[4] Like the worst of today's shelters, there was little privacy, and sanitary facilities, to the extent they existed, were meager.

By the beginning of the twentieth century, however, the station house was no longer viewed as a workable or appropriate solution. In a classic instance of out-of-sight, out-of-mind, the homeless of New York City were housed on a barge, a form of accommodation for the homeless that was considered as recently as 2002, when San Francisco administrators toured a fleet of mothballed World War II troop carriers moored nearby in the bay. As municipalities began to abandon their role in providing shelter for the homeless, charitable organizations took over, and the homeless shelter as we know it today emerged as a specific building type. Homeless shelters were variously called lodging houses, missions, or sanctuaries, and they were seen as a stopgap for those in the most extreme need; their design remained constant for a hundred years. The best known of the charitable organizations dedicated to assisting the homeless, the Salvation Army, was founded in 1865 by General William Booth to provide the homeless with spiritual guidance as well as emergency assistance; its first mission in New York City opened in 1891, and over the course of the following decade forty missions were founded in other locations throughout the country. The Salvation Army was among the first of the religious service organizations to view the homeless as having varying, specific needs and problems for which there were particular solutions.

The rescue missions were based in cities' skid row areas, and their primary beneficiaries were middle-aged men. Acceptance into a shelter was sometimes conditioned on the resident performing work—often demeaning make-work projects or hard labor—and changing his behavior. Behavioral reform, supported by an assumption that individuals could turn themselves around through the exercise of will, was enforced by a combination of lecturing, proselytizing, and mandatory chores. Little thought was given to how the shelter itself, and the experience of living in a shelter, might affect the individual and his ability to return to permanent housing.

Often the shelter was a secondary-use structure: an armory or a similarly large, open room designed for another purpose, usually assemblies. Design was limited to defining areas on the floor for beds, which were provided on a first-come, first-served basis. Throughout the century that followed, the essential character of shelters changed little; some were more humane, cleaner, or better safe-havens than others, but the perception that shelters for the homeless were "mean places" to be avoided at all costs is long-standing. The notion of "warehousing the poor" is more reality than metaphor; the first adult shelter I worked on in the mid-1990s was a converted warehouse (figure 6).

The first impression that these environments convey is one of unrelenting sameness and regimentation. Spaces and structures are unrelieved by visual variation; color, which might help mitigate the monotony, is entirely absent. Homeless shelters are the equivalent, transformed into interiors, of the endless rows of 1950s public-housing blocks. The larger the shelter, the more crushing is the impression of exposure and vulnerability that it conveys. Protection from the elements is the basis of all building, but creating a sense of security and

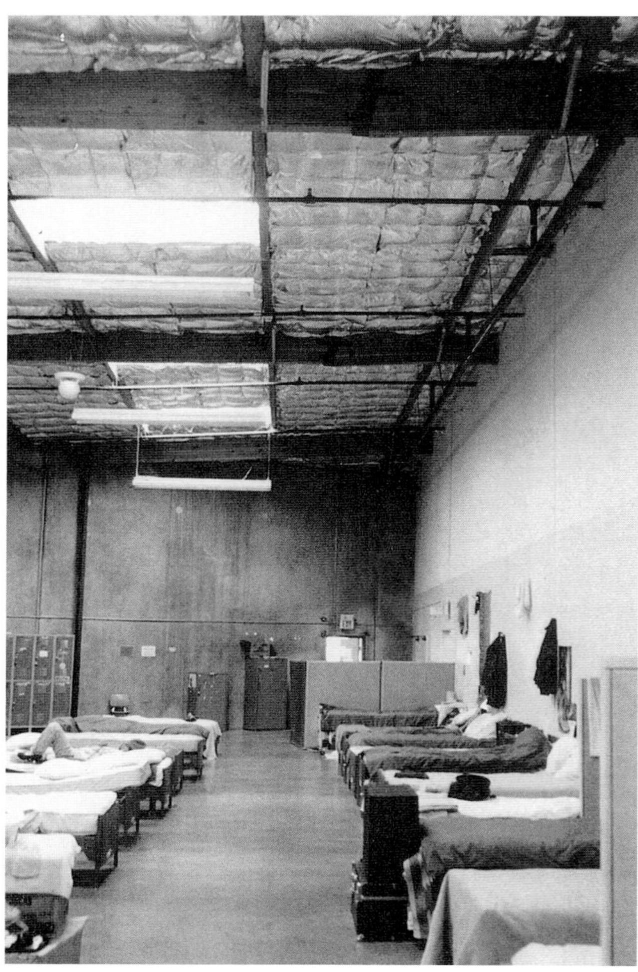

FIGURE 6 The Contra Costa County Adult Shelter, before renovation. The metaphor of warehousing the poor often reflects the reality of accommodations for the homeless.

refuge is a particular purview of good architecture. These shelter environments did, and often continue to do, the opposite.

While the charitable missions and shelters were (and remain) better managed than their municipal predecessors, accounts of shelter experiences are often horrifying testimony to the effect of shelters on their occupants. Regardless of whether this experience was universal, the reputation of homeless shelters was sufficient to make them a haven of last resort. In some sense their dehumanizing design was intentional: only the most desperate would enter shelters, and they wouldn't stay long. Even small gestures, such as privacy screens between beds, were deemed superfluous; the residents' desire for privacy was outweighed by the staff's need for clear sight lines to supervise the shelter's tougher occupants. Like all public or low-cost housing in the United States, shelters provided the barest minimum, with no amenities. Given the paucity of funding, moreover, doing the minimum was easy.

The demoralizing effect of a lack of privacy, personal territory, and individuality is amply attested to. Army barracks are intended to diminish the sense of self in order to encourage camaraderie and collective identity—to create a culture of "us against them," but these barracks operate in the context of a reward system, which offers (among other benefits) increased privacy as recruits rise through the ranks. The often-massive shelter dormitories provided no such assurances to their clients, and the residents saw the staff as guards. The size of some shelters exacerbated the problems. Some had a capacity of over four thousand. By the 1980s there were more than five thousand homeless shelters in the United States, collectively serving some twenty-five thousand people.[5] By 2000 New York City alone had an estimated homeless population of twenty-five thousand. Nonprofit service providers, funded largely by the government, operated the vast majority of these shelters.

LIFE IN THE SHELTERS

In spite of improvements in design and management over the past hundred years, shelter life is filled with challenges and hardships. The experience often strips the occupants of dignity, but how could it do otherwise? Institutionalization inculcates a resistance to acceptable social behavior to such an extent that the homeless either desperately avoid shelters or, once entering, create psychological walls (in the absence of real ones) in order to achieve some degree of personal privacy. Given such a choice, many prefer to stay on the street despite the physical challenges.

Sleep deprivation is only one of many problems associated with living in close proximity to many other people; a light stays on at all times, but worse are the constant night sounds: "There was snoring, coughing, sneezing, wheezing, retching, farting, cries from bad dreams and occasional weeping or seizures, talking aloud to oneself or to someone else who may or may not have been present, and always the movement to and from the bathroom."[6] Some wear earplugs or use sleep masks that cover the eyes, but there is a trade-off between the need to remain aware of one's surroundings to ensure personal security and the need to sleep. No degree of staff supervision or rules can replace the need for physical separation.

The close proximity of life in the shelters posed (and continues to pose) considerable risks to the residents' health and hygiene. Tuberculosis, pneumonia, and other airborne diseases were among the unseen hazards, and even now some shelters require proof of a negative TB test in order to gain admission. Recently some shelters (seeking a technological solution) have installed infrared lighting in air ducts to kill off airborne bacteria. Lice, flies, and mice were among the more readily apparent health hazards. Residents urinated or defecated in corners when the bathroom was too far away or too crowded—or simply as an act of defiance. The environment showed so little respect for the occupants that they reciprocated in kind.

Those unable to fend for themselves—the ill, the elderly, and the young—were often victims of assault. Whatever they might have of value could be easily stolen. The abusive drunk or the mentally ill might attack others without provocation. Segregating the populations would seem an obvious design and management solution, but this entailed more space, duplication of bathroom facilities, more supervisory staff—in short: more money.

Most shelters, lacking facilities for treatment, counseling, job training, or even amusement, required their residents to leave during the day. What do you do when there is no place to go? What do you wear when you don't have a change of clothes? Filling time—or killing it—between the shelter's hours of operation was just another of the challenges. Those who had work needed to find a place to fill the hours between the time they were required to leave the shelter and the time work started. While many just walked or sat outside in public places, others sought refuge indoors, often in public buildings, such as libraries, which (as advocates for the homeless often pointed out) they were legally entitled to use. In the early 1990s, I visited a new branch library in Las Vegas designed by the well-known architect Antoine Predock. The place was filled with homeless men, some asleep at tables with books upside down in front of them. They were unkempt, they smelled bad, and their presence became a deterrent to other patrons, but the library staff could do little.

As the profile of shelter residents began to change in the 1980s, so too did the variety and severity of the problems they faced in the shelters. The average age of shelter residents dropped from over fifty to the early thirties.[7] Individuals once housed in mental hospitals were now living in shelters, as were those recently released from prison, and shelters rapidly became overcrowded. A younger, tougher population, many of whom used drugs rather than alcohol, and an increasing number of women, some with children, made the warehouse approach even more unworkable.

The perception among the homeless of shelters as dangerous institutions can lead to distressing choices. Tommy (a pseudonym), a youth in his late teens, was living in Golden Gate Park in San Francisco. Outreach teams from a local youth services group were able to persuade him to come inside to meet with counselors, but only during the day. Even though they had a new shelter with space for him, he retreated to the park each night. During a harsh winter, Tommy got sick, and the clinic doctors told him he might not survive if he stayed in the park. He accepted the shelter bed, and his health improved. Only then, once he associated the shelter with his improving health, did he agree to stay long enough for the youth services program to help him in other ways. For Tommy, the mere idea of being inside, let alone in a communal facility, was so repugnant that he risked his health and safety not to go.[8]

THE MODERN SHELTER

Despite the perception that they were dangerous and unhealthy, by the 1980s the shelters that had provided refuge for nearly a century, like the public houses and police stations that preceded them, could no longer handle the increasing number of homeless. Nor could the volunteers and members of the clergy who had been leading the effort. Social scientists and social welfare professionals brought a more sophisticated knowledge and understanding to the needs of the diverse homeless population. A homeless system was emerging, and like other institutions or industries, it required buildings designed for very specific needs. Many of the facilities were new—not adapted from warehouses or armories—and they were large, sometimes exceeding 150,000 square feet, with sophisticated food service, security, and operating systems, built at a cost of up to $30 million.

In Los Angeles, often called the nation's homeless capital, several new homeless facilities were built in the downtown's skid row. Through financial incentives, the city encouraged service organizations to locate (or relocate) within this fifty-block area, concentrated on a street popularly known as "Mission Row." The intent was to circumscribe the problem, corral the homeless, and by doing so clean up areas of the downtown where new museums, corporate headquarters, and fancy hotels were located. As in the red-light zones of some European cities, the police ignore minor offenses on skid row, such as panhandling and vagrancy, that they would not tolerate a few blocks away.

Ambitious plans for new kinds of missions began to take shape in the late 1980s in Los Angeles and other metropolitan areas throughout the United States. In order to accommodate the numbers of homeless people, these modern-day shelters model themselves on professional businesses or institutions. Results—a healthy, healed, and changed individual—are the driving force of modern shelters, and although this goal was in fact that of shelters founded in the early twentieth century, the methods and the facilities themselves are a far cry from those of their predecessors. Among these new facilities is the Los Angeles Mission, initially designed by architect Scott MacGillivray and completed by Virginia Tanzmann in 1992 (figure 7). When it opened it was known as the Homeless Hilton. Here the homeless are "Our Friends and Neighbors," and the program is patterned after schools or colleges: clients are called students and those who work with them are faculty. The program, consisting of a set of educational modules, lasts two years and ends with a formal graduation ceremony. By 2002 a thousand people had graduated from the program.

The Los Angeles Mission treats the homeless not as an anonymous collective of people with problems that need to be overcome, but rather as individuals engaged in a process of education.[9] Learning here demands a commitment to spiritual awakening, the acquisition of life and academic skills, and physical well-being. Each component of its program has specifically designed areas within the complex: a chapel (the most prominent architectural element within the complex), a state-of-the-art computer classroom, a full-size gymnasium complete with bleachers and a scoreboard, a health clinic, a barbershop, and a weight room.

The facilities of the Los Angeles Mission itself are highly formalized, with clear points of entry and a progression from the most public areas to those with restricted access. Structure, figuratively and literally, defines the building. The homeless living on the street have little structure, and if they are to return to a productive life in society—which imposes norms of behavior—adherence to rules and regulations must be learned.

The initial shelter experience begins in a somewhat disconcerting manner, presuming that in order to change one must be stripped of all aspects of one's current life. It may seem dehumanizing, but here the objective is to have a fresh (and clean) start. The emergency shelter component of the mission offers beds to the homeless, who are given a number (first-come, first-served) that entitles them to a bed for five nights. Before receiving a meal, they must attend a chapel service; they are then taken upstairs, where they shower in a large communal facility, much like that of a school gym. Their clothes are stored, and they are issued clean pajamas and their bed number. The latter process takes some time, as there may be more than a hundred people seeking shelter; they wait on rows of stark wooden benches. The sleeping area is not much different from the homeless shelters of the past, with a room for staff that has a full view of the dormitory; the dormitory is filled with bunk beds, and lacks storage, nightstands, and privacy dividers. In some respects, however, the differences are salient; the dormitory is equipped with fire sprinklers, emergency exits, mechanical systems for heating and cooling, and it is extremely clean. But the basic profile of the dormitory—many people sleeping in one space—is that of conventional homeless shelters.

During these five days, the shelter's residents are encouraged to commit to a two-year program, known as the Urban Training Institute, ad-

FIGURE 7 The Los Angeles Mission. The gated forecourt, where the mission's clients line up for meals, beds, and social services, is the transition between the street and the shelter.

ministered in partnership with the Belmont Community Adult School. The program begins with a two-week orientation. During the first year, a disciplined regimen accounts for every hour; each day is divided into two-hour segments for learning, prayer, exercise, and work. Each resident is assigned a job in some component of the facility—food service, security, or maintenance—as a way to give residents a stake in the facility and its operation. Progress in the institute's program is rewarded by increasingly private and independent living spaces. The first stage is an open dormitory, divided into areas of six to eight beds; the next is a two-person room with a door. After more than a year, individuals leave the shelter for transitional housing administered by the mission.

In addition to progressively more independent living quarters, individuals enrolled in the Urban Training Institute receive other benefits over the course of the program. Clothing, including business suits, is donated to the mission, sorted by size, and maintained as a resource for graduating residents, or as work opportunities become available.

There is a bank on the premises, where residents can cash or deposit their public assistance or disability checks; on the street, most would have recourse only to local check-cashing facilities (which charge a fee, generally 10 percent of the check's value) and would have no alternative to carrying cash, which exposes them to risks. To obviate the intimidating environment of courthouses, certain infractions committed prior to enrollment can be resolved in a courtroom within the mission. Recognizing the dangers of skid row streets, the Los Angeles Mission provides what alternatives it can to leaving its grounds.

The mission's clients live and work in a sturdy, clean, and organized facility. With its large landscaped entry court, and cyclindrical chapel, the Los Angeles Mission is welcoming but not residential in character; it is, by design, an institutional building that conveys a message: "This was created to help you." What the resident sees, however, is only a small part of the mission's operation. Behind the residential elements is a labyrinth of utilities, offices, loading docks, storage rooms, and corridors, accessed by a sophisticated security system activated by electronic badges. The food management aspects alone are complex: tons of food, much of it donated, arrives by truck and is stored in dry goods rooms as well as in large refrigeration units. The mission serves more than twenty-five hundred meals a day, both to individuals enrolled in the mission's program and to the homeless from the streets seeking a meal. An entire floor houses administrative offices: human resources, volunteer coordinators, building operations staff, and, of course, fund raising. Staffed by a hundred paid employees and occupying a substantial building, the Los Angeles Mission is funded primarily by donations; obtaining money for its operations requires a professional fund-raising staff.

What the public sees, if they happen to find themselves on skid row, is a building that could easily be mistaken for a church complex or small college (figure 8). The Los Angeles Mission conveys a message of stability—that the institution is an enduring part of the community—and care has been taken to play down elements of its operations that might define it (to its residents and the public) as a conventional homeless shelter. Individuals seeking meals or access to overnight accommodation do not line up on the street, but within the gated courtyard, where the queue snakes around landscape planters.

Just two blocks from the Los Angeles Mission is the even larger Union Rescue Mission, designed by Herb Nadel, occupying approximately 240,000 square feet, and built at a cost of $29 million on land acquired with the help of the city. Established in 1891 by Union Oil Company founder Lyman Stewart, the Union Rescue Mission was once run from the back of a horse-drawn wagon from which a minister would exhort those who had wavered into sin to forsake liquor and come aboard the wagon as the first step. Lore has it that when asked where their drinking partners had gone, people were told they were "on the wagon"; if they succumbed again to alcohol they were said to have "fallen off the wagon." This immense shelter is a far cry from that wagon.

The Union Rescue Mission resembles its neighbor both programatically and in its religious grounding (attested to by a prominent cross at the entry), but its emphasis, as defined by its architecture, is somewhat different. It advertises its presence with architecturally bold and colorful elements (figure 9). Stairway towers, constructed of masonry blocks, form large buttresses against the bulk of the building, conveying a sense of solidity and strength. The interior of the complex is less highly finished: air ducts are left exposed, and the

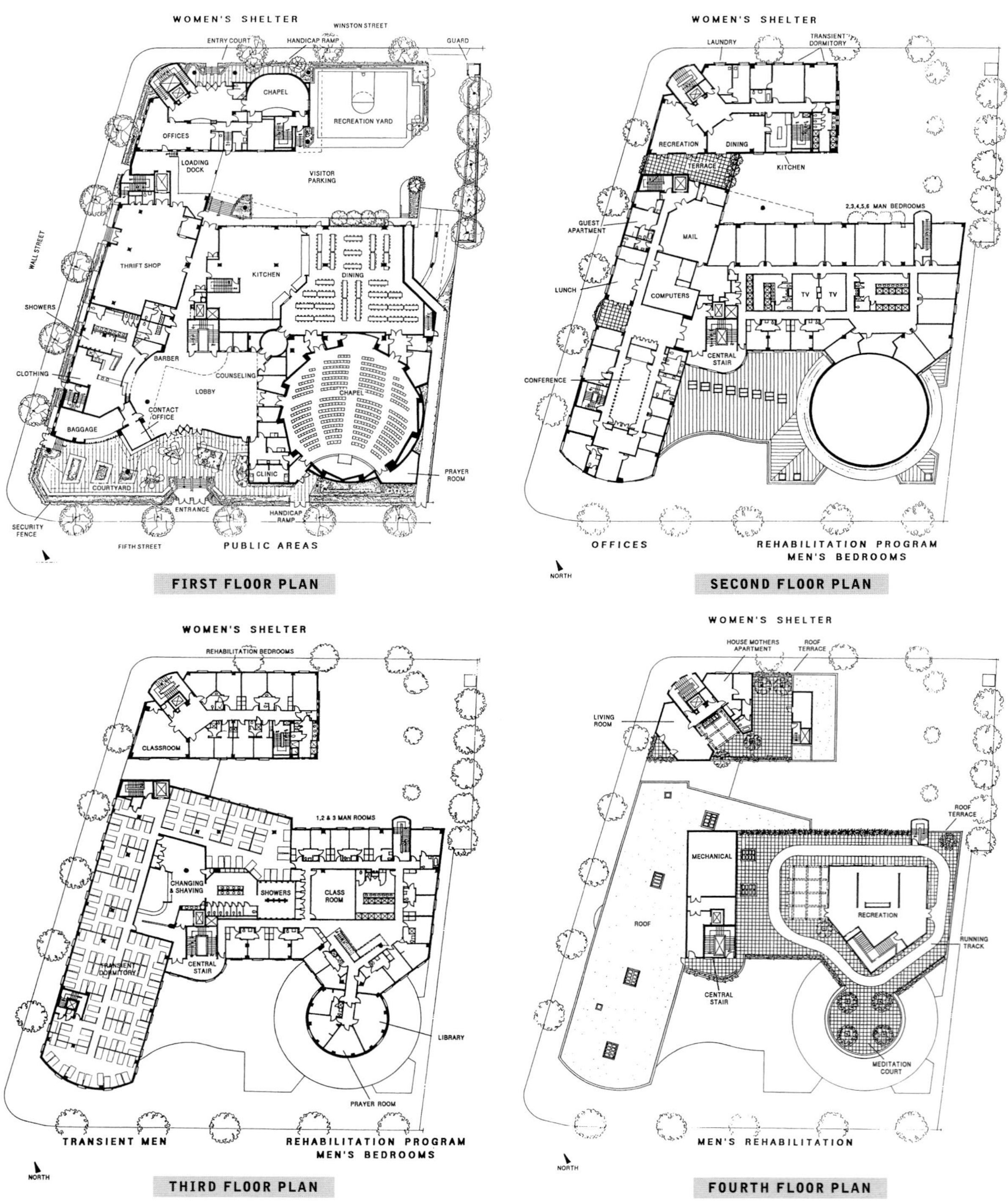

FIGURE 8 The plans of the Los Angeles Mission. The chapel, with an entrance directly on the courtyard, is the most prominent element of the complex.

FIGURE 9 The front of the Union Rescue Mission facing San Pedro Street.

floors are nearly all bare concrete. These design decisions were partly budget-based (although the Union Rescue Mission complex is larger and newer than the Los Angeles Mission, its construction cost slightly less), but it is also a conceptual decision. This message is: "We are here to help, but this is not your home."[10]

Whereas the Los Angeles Mission accommodates a small population of women without children in a separate building, the Union Rescue Mission has a large population of women, many with young children—a reflection of how rapidly the demographics of homelessness changed between 1992, when the Los Angeles Mission opened, and 1994, when the Union Rescue Mission was completed. The need to accommodate women and children, as well as homeless men, raised programmatic and architectural complexities in the mission's design (figures 10 and 11). Men and women are segregated even to the extent of separate waiting courtyards and day rooms, situated at the back of the complex (the public entrance gives on the street). The gender distribution of the mission's population has changed even over the space of six years, and the wall separating the day rooms has been moved as a consequence to enlarge the size of the women's facility. Meals are served in a single large dining area, but men and women (together with their children) eat at separate times.

The staffing of the Union Rescue Mission's two emergency dormitories (which can accommodate up to 450 people) is one indication of the extent to which gender underlies differences in the needs of the homeless. It takes one person to get several

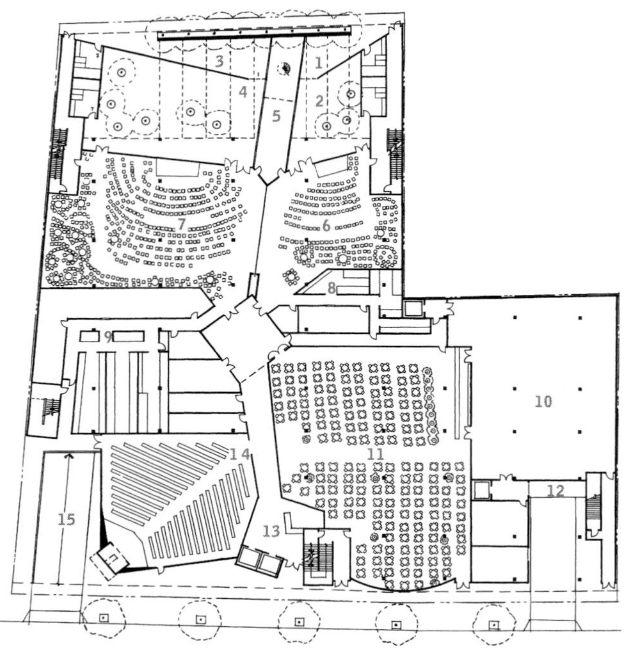

FIRST FLOOR

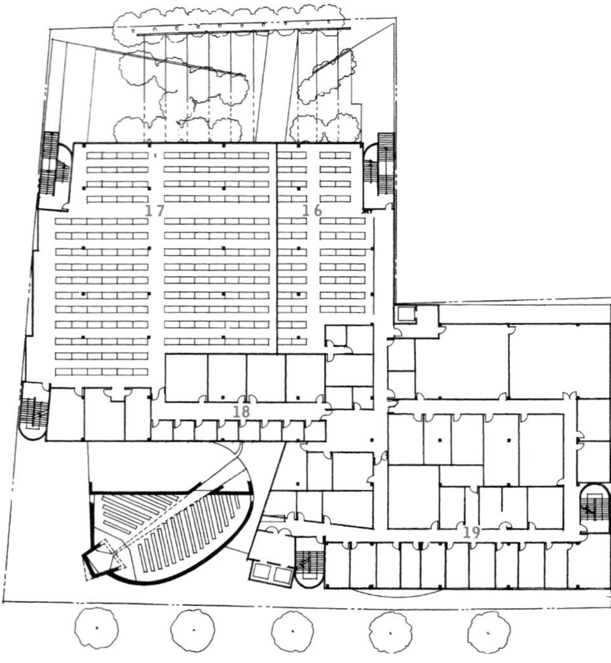

SECOND FLOOR

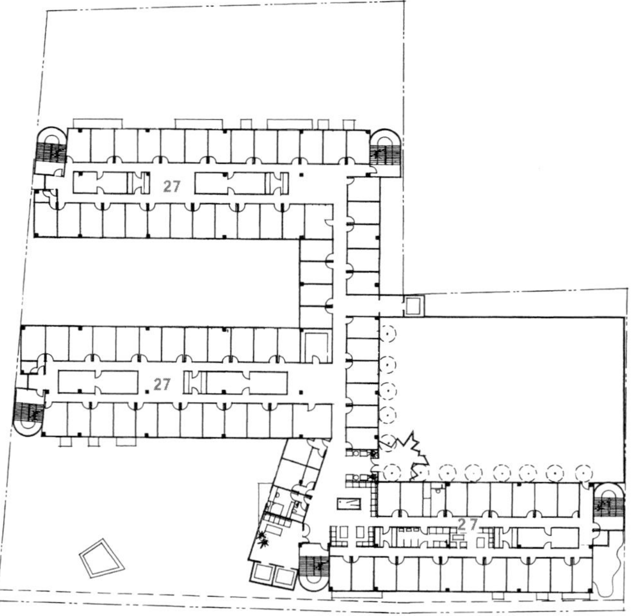

FIFTH FLOOR

FIGURE 10 The plans of the Union Rescue Mission *(here and opposite)*.

KEY	
1 Women's outer courtyard	15 Ramp to parking
2 Women's inner courtyard	16 Women's guest dorm
3 Men's outer courtyard	17 Men's guest dorm
4 Men's inner courtyard	18 Clinic
5 Guest reception/referral	19 Administration
6 Women's recreation	20 Men's recovery program
7 Men's recreation	21 Gymnasium/multipurpose
8 Women's hygiene	22 Men's detox
9 Men's hygiene	23 Women's recovery program
10 Kitchen	24 Youth activity
11 Guest dining	25 Learning center
12 Service	26 Women's detox
13 Lobby	27 Staff housing
14 Chapel	

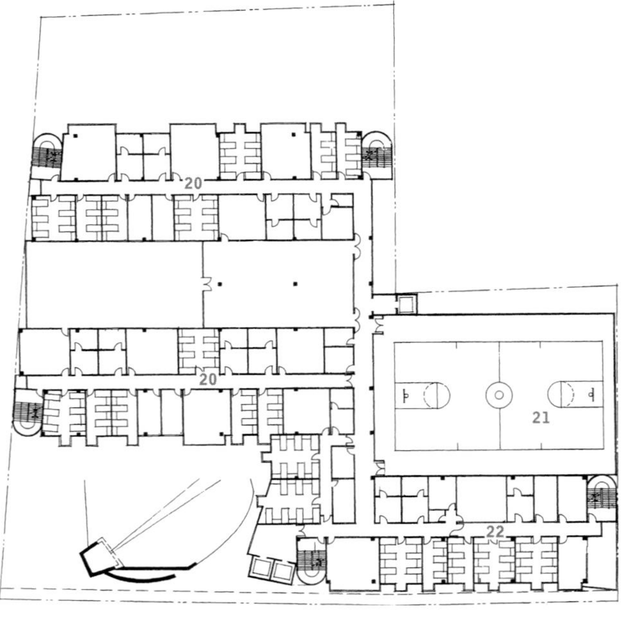

THIRD FLOOR

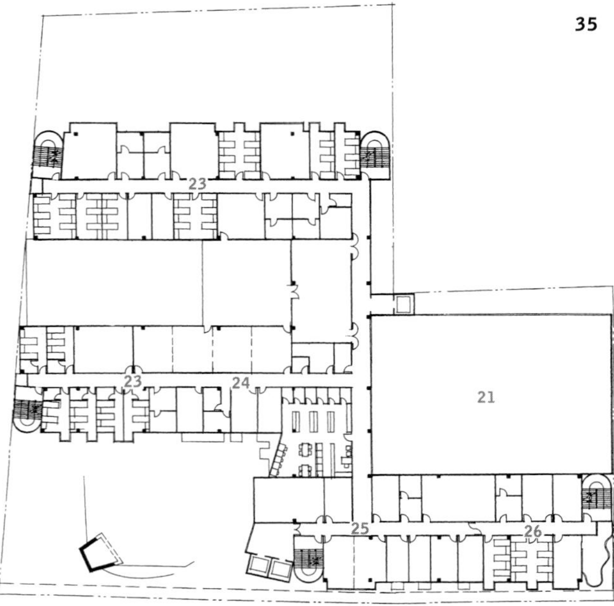

FOURTH FLOOR

hundred men to get to their beds before the lights are dimmed; as many as seven staffers are needed to get a hundred women to settle in. The women who come to the shelter are extremely traumatized by their experience of homelessness; many have been physically or sexually abused; they are unused to sharing accommodation with so many people, and as a consequence tend to feel extremely vulnerable. Staffers often take time to sit with the women in order to put them at ease so that they can rest.

The Union Rescue Mission offers its clients a full array of programs, classrooms, and exercise spaces within its 240,000 square feet. Among them is a large clinic run by the School of Nursing of the University of California, Los Angeles, and a dental clinic run by the University of Southern California's School of Dentistry. The arrangement benefits both the shelter's residents and those providing the services: the mission's residents receive professional care, while the university's students gain practical experience, as well as the opportunity to serve a community that has little access to (but much need of) medical care.

One section of a floor within the mission's complex is reserved for guests and volunteers who want to learn about homelessness. Groups stay at the mission, often for a weekend, and participate in various aspects of its operations. This element of the Union Rescue Mission's programs seeks to educate the public about homelessness and to draw in potential donors. Unfortunately, the pressure to accommodate more homeless people has already reduced the size of this space.

The Los Angeles Mission and the Union Rescue Mission seek to do far more than simply

FIGURE 11 The bold forms of the Union Rescue Mission in Los Angeles define it as a stable and important facility. The facility's entrance on San Julian Street, illustrated here, includes a courtyard, with separate entries for men and women.

"contain" the homeless (as early twentieth-century shelters tended to do); the sophistication of their programs, together with the size of the two facilities, is reflected in the complexity of their design. Designing the two complexes was an opportunity for the architects to participate in projects that have an important social component, but these were also major commissions, with substantial fees.[11] The Los Angeles Mission and the Union Rescue Mission represent the latest thinking in shelters. They could not have been done without architects. Much of the funding for these projects was provided by wealthy, high-profile donors (the women's wing of the Los Angeles Rescue Mission is named for Anne Douglas, wife of the actor Kirk Douglas and mother of the actor and producer Michael Douglas). In this sense the patronage system continues for architects, but with more magnanimous results.

FLOPS, RESIDENTIAL HOTELS, AND LODGING HOUSES

Flops and inexpensive lodging houses catered to individuals with limited funds seeking an alternative to shelters. During the Great Depression, cheap lodging houses were common in most American cities, particularly in New York, where there were as many as a hundred "cubicle hotels" in the Bowery alone. These facilities took several forms within a basic loft building, the main distinction being the extent of privacy afforded to the residents: the more money, the more solitude. Even today in New York, where a few of the lodging houses remain in operation, a cubicle costs only $4.50 a night. Although lodging houses, residential hotels, and flops are now generally referred to synonymously under the rubric of "flophouse," Paul Groth, in his thorough study of cheap housing in the United States, *Living Downtown,* distinguishes costs and levels of amenities within lodging houses, which offered their residents either private rooms, a bed in a cubicle, or a bed in a ward.[12] Sometimes a single building offered all three arrangements, each on a different floor, but more often they were distinct buildings, each targeting a different clientele.

THE FLOPHOUSE

The least expensive of the three options was the open ward, comparable to an army barracks or to the shelters, which offered a bed for the night or just a space on the floor. The next step up was the cubicle. The interior of the cubicle lodging house was split into small booths (like work cubicles in an open-plan office), which residents called cages, usually five feet by seven, but sometimes as small as four feet by six (figure 12). Each cubicle had a locking door, but no ceiling; the top was roofed with chicken wire that kept out the "crawlers" or "lush divers" who might climb over the walls to steal the belongings of the sleeping or unconscious resident (figure 13). The wire also kept people from occupying a cubicle without paying, and it provided a bit of ventilation and access (albeit minimal) to light. Cubicle hotels sometimes comprised as many as six floors, each floor furnished with a single bathroom. A clerk sat in a booth at the foot of a long stairway winding down from the upper floors to the street, but the hotels had no lobby or public facilities to speak of; the ground floor might be occupied by a saloon or a tattoo parlor, which was entered from the street. Men who sought privacy, anonymity, and relative freedom from rules and regulations lived in the flops. These guys just wanted to be left alone.

Flops and lodging houses were plagued by safety hazards that would be impermissible under today's building codes. Emergency access was limited, and bathroom or bathing facilities were insufficient for the number of residents. Windows were often situated only at the front and rear, separated by a wide expanse of floor. The walls of the cubicles blocked most of the light or ventilation that a window might afford, but few of the boxes were near a window anyway. While the flops may have satisfied the lax codes of their era, they only barely did so, and their tough residents were in any event undemanding. The facilities would have needed to be well managed and maintained to provide anything more than seedy accommodation, and with a staff often limited to a single employee, who observed the coming and goings from his ground-floor cage, they were not.

Even today, a sense of foreboding greets visitors stepping out of the stairway into the floor that houses the flophouse cubicles, rendered more sinister when one begins to navigate its labyrinth of narrow blind passageways. Even in daytime, light from the windows or ceiling fixtures only barely penetrates the gloom, and the darkness masks the filth of the floors and the walls of the boxes. Other senses make the squalor all too evident: the air is stale, the odd smell compounded of disinfectant and perspiration. Muffled sounds of habitation penetrate the silence. You know that people are there, but you don't know who they are or where they are.

It is an insidious miracle that such places could continue to flourish in a time of housing reform and toughened building codes, but an uneasy accommodation existed between landlords and municipal regulators. Flops were lucrative businesses

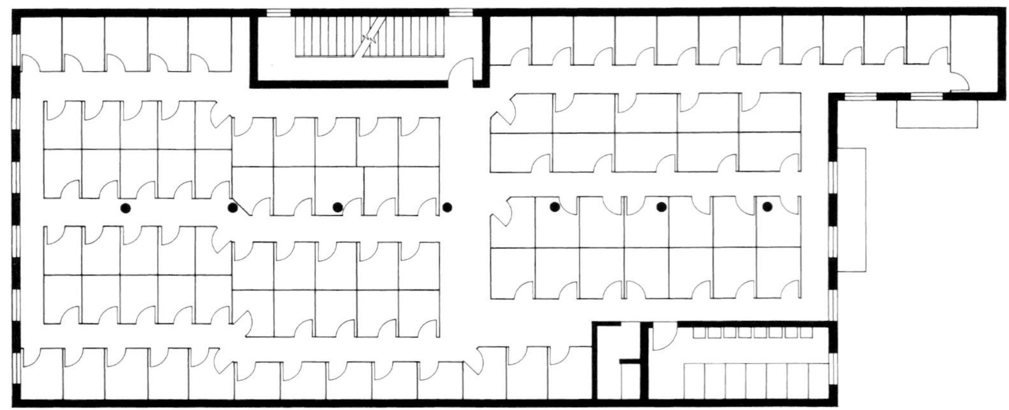

FIGURE 12 The floor plan of a New York City flophouse. The design is intended to make maximum use of the loft space; each floor contains a single stairway and bathroom, serving more than ninety residents.

FIGURE 13 Residents of New York City flophouses, like the one illustrated here, had private rooms; walls that stopped several feet short of the ceiling provided limited air circulation.

that required little initial investment, and they served to remove the most downtrodden from the streets and to keep them isolated in a discrete part of town. At the height of the Depression, the flops in New York City's Bowery housed as many as 75,000 men.[13] The waning of their popularity reflected the postwar economic upturn in the United States. World War II essentially ended the era of flophouses; single men went off to war and returned to an array of social programs that made this type of housing less necessary. By the middle of the twentieth century, stricter building codes, reduced need, and increased property values had all but eliminated the flophouse.

In 2003 there were eight surviving flophouses in New York, a number that is certain to diminish in coming years. But as many as a thousand men avoid homelessness within them in spite of the grim conditions. Who lives there now? In their book *Flophouse,* David Isay and Stacy Abramson profile the residents, documenting the passing of this housing type while acknowledging that there are those for whom this housing is serving a need. Each resident, in his own words, describes his trip to the flop.

> I'm Robert Conners. Bobby Conner. Bobby O'Conner. Bobby Conners. I'm a heroin user and pill-head, and I have an attention deficit disorder—hyperactivity with rapid speech. I'm forty-four, grew up in Bay Ridge, Brooklyn—a nice neighborhood. And I'm an ironworker by trade. I come from a whole family of ironworkers—my father was an ironworker, my brothers are ironworkers. I worked on every bridge in New York. I busted rivets out for seventeen years, and I was considered one of the best rivet-busters in New York City. An authority. To cut to the chase, at the age of thirty-five I had the world by the balls: I worked for the Department of Transportation, I bought stocks on the NASDAQ, I was sober. So I said to myself: "I'm working on bridges, I'm making fifty-two grand a year—I can handle this job drunk." And that's exactly what I did. I worked for years on the bridges—drunk and popping pills.
>
> At the age of thirty-eight I started going to the Providence Hotel out of convenience. I was working on the Williamsburg Bridge and I said, "I can go to the hotel dirty, wake up with a hangover, shower, and go to work." I was into pills at the time: Percocet, Darvocet, benzos—the whole nine yards. Anyway, it got out of hand. I took a seizure, and I fell off the Williamsburg Bridge and landed in the net. I blamed it on MSG and the Chinese food, but my boss wasn't going for it, so I lost my job.
>
> I'm optimistic about getting it together. I read the Bible every day, and I get on my knees and pray to God to end this obsession with drugs. I go to a church every night—even under the influence. I've never lost my union card, and my whole family's rooting for me, even though I've burned a lot of bridges. I'm only forty-four, I have no criminal record, and you know, I consider myself—people tell me anyway—"You're a hell of a nice guy." They tell me, "Bobby you seem like a stand-up guy—what the fuck is the problem? Can't you get it together?"[14]

He died shortly after making this statement.

FLOPHOUSE REDUX

It is hard to imagine that so dreadful a living environment, with so fraught a history, could be considered viable today. Under the leadership of its founder and executive director, Rosanne Haggerty, however, the nonprofit Common Ground Community in New York is reconceptualizing the cubicle hotel as an alternative for those who are both service- and shelter-resistant. Common Ground's clients—mostly male and middle-aged—are very much like those who inhabited the flops a century ago: they want privacy, no questions, and minimal rules. If they cannot have these, they would rather be on the streets. Haggerty believes that providing an alternative to the streets for these individuals can lead to something better, particularly if strong management and services are provided on-site.[15]

Haggerty calls the resuscitated flop "First Step Housing"; the idea itself, and its execution, reflects a belief in the power of good design. Haggerty accounts for the demise of the cubicle hotel as "more a failure of imagination on our part than anything imbedded in the model."[16] Common Ground's rethinking of cubicle hotels was based on years of study (by Haggerty and others) into small-space living environments throughout the world, including the Japanese "capsule hotels," where businessmen slide into drawerlike beds. Planning research included interviews with potential residents, who commented on pictures of various options (such as Amtrak sleepers and small cabins). Although the research confirmed that the cubicle hotel might be viable, it provided little direction as to form:

> It was fascinating to me how hardwired certain images of home are into our collective psyche. You'd ask someone who had been living on the street for years—probably always in the city—to draw a picture of what they had in mind, and they would draw something like a kindergartner's picture of home, a little pitched-roof thing. So our first iteration of the First Step was that: It looked like Thoreau's cabin.[17]

Common Ground purchased the hundred-year-old Andrews Hotel as the setting for First Step and began working with two New York architects, Marguerite McGoldrick and Gans + Jelacic. Someone who said, "You don't want it to be a dollhouse, but you don't want it to be a cell either," voiced the design dilemma.[18] After several iterations, including the archetypal cabin version, the architects developed an ingenious demountable cubicle that accommodates the needs of the residents, the demands of the building code, and budgetary constraints (figures 14 and 15). Each cubicle is six and a half feet by eight in plan, and eight feet high. The cubicle's major structural component is an extruded piece of aluminum that is a cruciform in section, used at each corner of the box, both horizontally and vertically, to provide rigidity and to anchor the wall panels, which are bolted to the flanges. A sliding door hangs from the flange. Inside there is a closet with a perforated metal door that provides ventilation (clothes are rarely washed); a desk and a bed are attached to an aluminum rail, affixed to the panels. One of the advantages of a system of this type is that damaged or worn elements can be easily replaced. Maintenance was rare in the original cubicle hotels; the hope is that residents of First Step will respect the environment if it is well cared for.

Like the cubicles in the early twentieth-century flops, the ceilings of the First Step cubicles are not completely enclosed. This is intended in part to contain costs and provide ventilation, but it also reflects building code requirements for fire sprinklers: were the tops solid, each cubicle would require a separate sprinkler head. Instead, the top is perforated metal (the same material used on the closet doors), and the number and size of holes were determined by the fire officials. The doors to the cubicles are similarly designed to accommodate use and regulatory requirements: sliding doors do not obstruct the passageways or the interior space (as would be the case if they swung outward or inward), and they can be opened by those in wheelchairs without the clearance that hinged

FIGURE 14 The flophouse cubicle redux. First Step Housing's module features elegant detailing, flexibility, privacy, and safety.

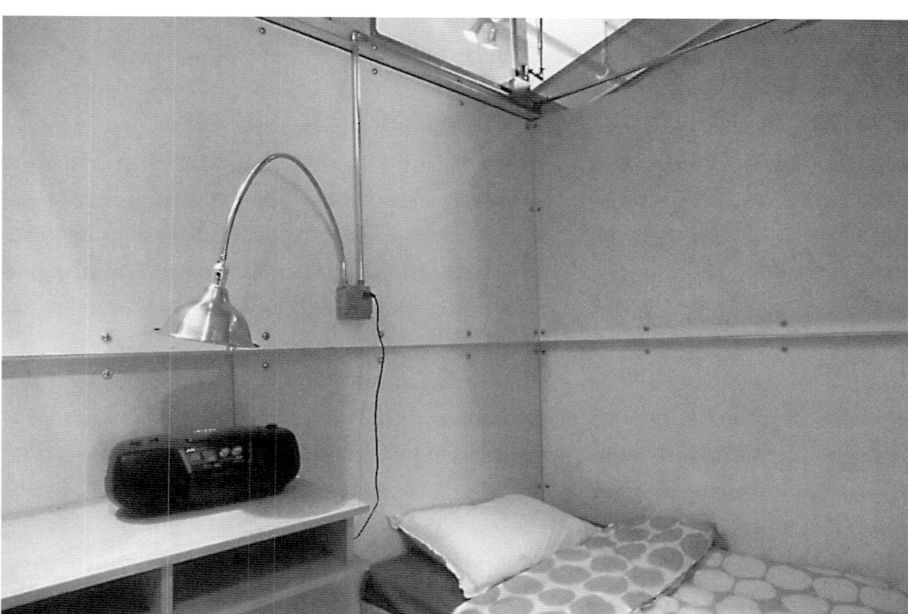

FIGURE 15 The flanges on which the First Step module is assembled also anchor the desks and beds to the facility's walls.

doors would require. The configuration of the cubicles on the floors of the building is flexible. They can be linked together in a line, or they can be clustered in other configurations. Two people can reconfigure several in less than a day. The cost of each cubicle is approximately $3,500, but, as with any manufactured product, there are economies of scale. The ability to ship the units flat and to assemble them on-site may make them feasible in other contexts, reducing their unit cost as accommodations for the homeless.

The goal of First Step is to provide housing for individuals who would otherwise fall outside the homeless safety net. The program's approach, however, has ignited a debate: Does this form of housing perpetuate a type that should rightfully have become extinct years ago, or does it provide a necessary service? In the abstract, I believe that we should strive to upgrade housing and make it more accessible and affordable, but my work with the homeless has led me to the same conclusion as that of Rosanne Haggerty: making places that are dignified, providing options for people who may have had no options at all, and attracting the homeless to accommodations that offer opportunities to take advantage of ancillary social services is a worthy approach.

ROOMING HOUSES AND RESIDENTIAL HOTELS

Residential hotels offered individuals with some income an alternative to shelters and flophouses. These facilities were designed not for tourists but rather for manufacturing and construction laborers working in cities. Whereas shelters, flops, and lodging houses were more often than not converted from other uses, residential hotels were built expressly for this purpose; as a result, form followed function and the hotels satisfied building codes. The most distinctive plan element was the repetitive light well (figure 16), which ensured that each room had access to some natural light and a modicum of ventilation. The buildings' architects sometimes crafted ingenious solutions to the challenge of providing a window in each unit of the tightly packed series of rooms that composed each floor.

Rooming houses and residential hotels of the early 1900s were more akin to dormitories than to tourist hotels (at the higher end of the scale) or to flophouses (at the lower end). Each resident had a private room, but the bath was shared—often with as many as twenty-five others. Each room shared a light well with as many as three other rooms on each floor (and the building generally comprised several floors), so there was little acoustical isolation. The interior walls were uninsulated, and the penetration of sound between adjoining rooms mooted the nominal privacy of individual rooms.

Paul Groth, in a personal account of living in a residential hotel, describes how the residents are drawn into the patterns of other people's lives as a response to the architecture. Everyone sharing a light well knows who watches what television shows; one knows when others arise to go to work and thus can avoid showering or using the bathroom at those times.[19] Despite these inconveniences, rooming houses and residential hotels were far better (for those who could afford them) than the cheaper options. Each room usually contained a sink, a desk and chair, and a wardrobe; there was some form of emergency access; most of these facilities contained a real lobby, a shared living room, and sometimes a dining room as well.

Rooming houses and residential hotels also provided accommodation for single working women, even in rough neighborhoods. Housing reformers frowned on this type of group living as an affront to family life, and they were particu-

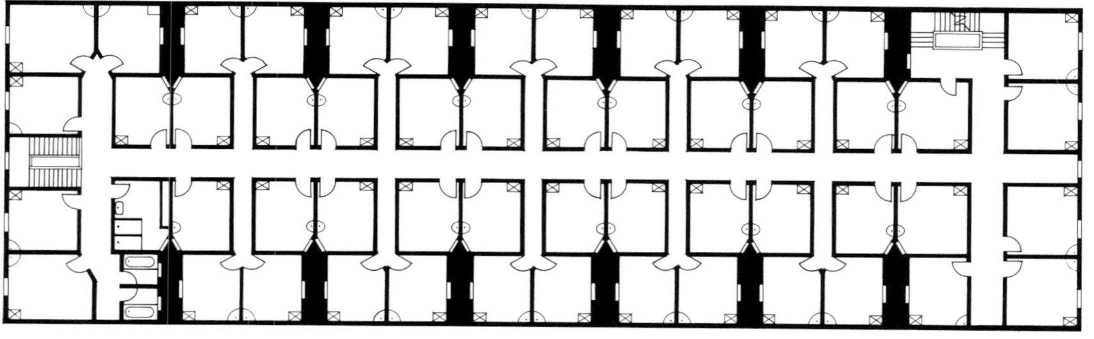

FIGURE 16 Although they are tightly packed to make maximum use of the space, each room in this San Francisco rooming house (1906) contains a window; those on the interior overlook an airshaft.

larly opposed to such arrangements for women, for they saw the rooming house as an obstacle to becoming a proper homemaker. Yet for those unmarried individuals who needed (or wanted) to live and work in cities, the rooming house was proper, safe, and economical. The relatively low numbers of homeless women in American cities during the early twentieth century resulted in part from the availability of the YWCA and accommodations such as these.

As jobs grew scarce, however, the profile of these facilities' residents changed. By mid-century, many residential hotels were occupied by the poor or elderly on fixed incomes (either from disability pay or retirement). Although the hotels tended to be situated in the seedier parts of town, their residents nonetheless had access to public transportation and other facilities; when the neighborhoods declined, those living in the hotels were less willing to venture out. These hotels, which did much to establish the visual character of cities, began to disappear as urban renewal took place at mid-century. We now lament the passing of these structures, for their mid-rise successors have changed the scale and varied the visual texture of streetscapes. Of those that survive, many have been converted to expensive condominiums; their often-gracious facades, combined with large flexible floor plans, make them attractive for loft-type housing.

The quality of the rooming house was (and remains) more a function of its management than of its design. The degree to which behavior is monitored and residency conditioned on adherence to basic rules, as well as the extent of cleaning and maintenance, distinguishes those that are good places to live, way stations to something better, or one step from homelessness. Two young men with whom I spoke, who now live in a specially designed facility for those with HIV/AIDS, described the conditions in several San Francisco residential hotels where they lived while awaiting space in this new housing. In some of the worst places, their rooms were infested with cockroaches and the walls of the common bathroom smeared with feces. They were often woken by individuals pounding on their door, offering to sell them crack. The rent for these facilities (paid by a nonprofit service group) was as much as $100 a week; better-managed accommodations cost $265 per week.[20]

THE SRO—THE NEW ROOMING HOUSE

The single room occupancy hotel (SRO) is a version of the rooming house, but rooms in such hotels were often furnished with private bathrooms and modest cooking facilities (sometimes, even a fully equipped kitchen). The SRO thus resembles the "palace" hotels of the early 1900s, or extended-stay business hotels of the present day. One reason for the successful reemergence of SROs is that many survive, albeit in poor condition, and can be acquired and renovated by nonprofit organizations. Developers have discerned an emerging market among lower-income individuals (including the young). New buildings, many designed by some of the nation's best architects, have been constructed in several downtowns. Housing shortages in cities throughout the United States spurred the relaxation of zoning regulations and building codes, which had discouraged investment in SROs, as well as capital improvements. Victorian standards proffered by reformers of the late nineteenth and early twentieth century were limited to forms of housing deemed socially acceptable: mainly houses or fully equipped apartments. By the late twentieth century, however, society had become more tolerant of various types of living arrangements and the dwellings that accommodated them.

The first architect to gain national acclaim for new SROs was Rob Wellington Quigley in San Diego. Working with developers Chris Mortenson and Bud Fischer in the early 1990s, Quigley created several architecturally noteworthy SROs, many of which have garnered national design awards. The best known is 202 Island Inn, a bold and colorful building knitted into an existing downtown district (figure 17). While many architects design multifamily housing, Quigley made the SRO a particularly respectable architectural endeavor. Many others have followed, and SROs have been constructed in virtually every large American city.

At the higher end of the spectrum are self-contained studio apartments, marketed to low-income hourly workers. A new Quigley project in Las Vegas—Campaige Place—targets single, hourly wage earners working in the service sector, who need access to public transportation. Units, with all furniture built-in, rent for $500 per month.[21]

Some new-generation SROs resemble their boardinghouse predecessors: the bathrooms are shared, but individual units have their own sink. Each floor may have a common room and a shared kitchen. In the Downtown Women's Center in Los Angeles, designed by architect Brenda Levin, shared bathrooms form a core at the center of each floor, surrounded by a U-shaped hallway that contains individual rooms; a lounge at the hallway's open end overlooks the street; adjacent to the lounge is a kitchen used by the floor's residents. The residents of each floor have formed a small community, often cooking meals together and assisting one another, much as neighbors would do.

Other SROs resemble college dormitories, lacking kitchen facilities, with a common bathroom shared among several units. Such SROs are transitional housing, offering safe and comfortable accommodation to those who might otherwise be on the streets. Among the new versions of this type of SRO is the Boyd Hotel in Los Angeles by Koning-Eizenberg Architects, built in 1996 (figures 18 and 19). Most SROs contain a lobby that functions as an extended living room; some contain a library as well. At the higher end, there may be amenities such as a workout room and patio.

There is nothing unique about these buildings. More often than not they comprise a simple arrangement of replicated rooms along both sides

FIGURE 17 202 Island Inn, San Diego. Their dynamic architecture, signaled here by a prominent entry, makes this new generation of SROs an attractive low-cost housing alternative.

of a corridor. But they are important buildings nonetheless, not only because they fulfill a housing need, but also because they are revitalizing urban areas that have been left to decay for decades. They have a prominent front door, often with an awning; many have lobbies with large windows facing the street, and their three- or four-story facades fit comfortably within urban neighborhoods just outside the city's core. To compensate for the low rents, developers often include small commercial spaces on the ground floor. Rather than the tattoo parlors and saloons of their predecessors, however, these are more often service facilities, retail stores, or coffee shops that cater to the building's residents as well as to residents of the neighborhood. These new residential hotels are a friendly and respectable presence, and so too, by association, are their occupants.

Nevertheless many with whom I spoke in the shelters feel that the SRO is not the best housing type for those graduating to permanent dwellings.

FIGURE 18 The entrance to the Boyd Hotel, Los Angeles.

They express concern that individuals who have completed rigorous programs within shelters have regained a sense of community, or at least a means of reestablishing social networks, and that the graduates of these programs, living in a private room in an SRO, may grow isolated and relapse into behaviors and habits that contributed to homelessness. In the latter case, SROs with common facilities may be most appropriate, and in many cases these buildings have a restaurant-style kitchen and meals are taken communally. This type of situation is particularly valuable for individuals with disabilities, who may not be able to cook for themselves.

THE STREETS

Shelters and the various forms of housing just described are generally considered solutions for short-term or temporary homelessness. Treating homelessness as an emergency makes otherwise intolerable housing conditions acceptable; when people take refuge in a local gymnasium after a natural disaster, they do so knowing that they will soon

FIGURE 19 The lobby of the Boyd Hotel, Los Angeles.

find better and permanent housing. Innovative, easily constructed, and cost-effective emergency habitations, such as modular units, are often used as temporary housing for victims of disaster. After the 1906 earthquake and fire in San Francisco, thousands were housed in cottages set up in parks.

ALONE ON THE STREETS

Some, including many architects, see homelessness as a similar emergency, provoked by social forces, that can be alleviated through resourcefulness and good design.[22] Some believe that in certain instances homeless people *choose* to live as transients; they may be eccentric, maladjusted, or peculiar, but they are neither criminal, nor dangerous, nor mentally ill. We should just let them live in peace and in a way that is secure, safe, and hygienic.

Over the past twenty years, several architects have created prototype accommodations for individuals who prefer to live on the streets. Some are as rudimentary as scored corrugated cardboard that can be easily transported and configured into

FIGURE 20 The self-contained sleeping module of Donald MacDonald's innovative City Sleeper, shown here in San Francisco, can be closed and locked during the day. Holes on the sides provide ventilation.

a tentlike cover. Others are more conventional, basically mini-houses, factory-made and modular, modeled on the precedent of the crisis cottage. In 1987 San Francisco architect Donald MacDonald put his considerable housing design skills to work for the group of homeless men who inhabited the parking lot next to his office. After discussions with them in which they made it clear that a clean, warm place to sleep was all they needed or wanted, MacDonald created his "City Sleeper," an elegant plywood container just large enough for a person to crawl into and recline (figure 20).

Essentially a piece of outdoor cabinetry, the City Sleeper had many thoughtful features. The doorway lifted up, like the back of a station wagon, so that the occupant could sit facing out, while protected from rain or sun. Inside were a foam mattress and some shelves; a window and two small openings—

FIGURE 21 The simple design of the Mad Houser's cabin keeps production costs low and facilitates rapid assembly.

one low and one high—ensured ventilation. The entire device was raised off the ground, supported on car jacks that could be adjusted to make the unit level. MacDonald proposed setting up City Sleepers in areas that the homeless already occupied—vacant lots or under bridges—with the stipulation that only a few would be situated in any one place. Aggregating too many City Sleepers in one place, he argued, would discourage use of the devices, since his clients just wanted to be left alone, and the larger the community, the greater the risk of disputes over squatting rights. The street homeless are generally antisocial, tolerating only a small band of like-minded people, who look out for one another. MacDonald had assumed that the City Sleepers would be accepted by municipal authorities, and that municipalities would even set up portable toilets near the structures. His vision never came to pass, however, and ultimately the structures were removed.

Other, less elegant designs were executed by the Mad Housers, a group of recent graduates from architectural degree programs, lawyers, and homeless advocates. They began by building 8-foot plywood cubes, with sloping tops to shed rain, during weekends in Atlanta; each could be assembled in as little as seventeen minutes (figure 21). These were trucked to sites within the city, and left for the homeless to occupy, sometimes for as long as several months, after which they were abandoned. Over the years the structures have become more sophisticated, and the Mad Housers' approach, which now includes working with other groups to connect their clients to social services, has been adopted by groups in other cities. The group's early pronouncements reflect the Mad Housers' "guerrilla building" approach to providing housing for street people: "The dignity of a man who owns a house, albeit minimal and illegal, over a man who sleeps on the ground . . . or the legitimizing effect of sleeping in a structure rather than stealing a nap on a park bench, all contribute to the individual, helping him to improve his own circumstances."[23]

In cities throughout the country similar designs emerged, nearly all under the auspices of architects, designers, or artists. These structures were welcomed by the homeless, but the response of municipal officials and police, who were obligated to uphold building regulations and vagrancy laws, ranged from grudging tolerance to outrage. Although the structures provided an alternative form of shelter for many on the street, they did not meet building codes, and their placement violated zoning ordinances.

ENCAMPMENTS

In cities all across the country, teams of police conduct periodic sweeps of homeless encampments in parks, under bridges, or in alleys, waking up the residents and moving them out. The areas are filthy, littered with human waste and drug paraphernalia, and the police are quickly followed by public works teams, which power-wash the area. Within a few days, or even a few hours, the homeless return to a sanitized place; they sometimes joke about having called for housekeeping. The ritual is expensive, and it often gives rise to mutual hostility.

Well-hidden encampments—concealed, for example, in a thickly planted corner of a park—usually last longer. One of the most surreal instances (captured in the documentary film *Dark Days*) was a group of dwellings, some with extensive furniture and cooking facilities, set up in train tunnels beneath New York City; by tapping into freshwater pipes and splicing into electrical lines, many of these squats lasted undisturbed for as long as twenty years. New York City has had other homeless encampments throughout its history; during the mid-1800s, for example, much of Central Park was inhabited by squatters.

MacDonald's understanding was that the street homeless wanted small, loose, and informal social networks. Yet there have been several attempts recently—some with skeptical but official acceptance—to create larger homeless encampments. Underlying many of these initiatives is an attempt to restore to the homeless a sense of dignity and control through the process of collaboration and self-governance that such a community effort demands. With names like Justiceville, Dignity Village, or Love Camp, many of these settlements include architects and builders among their supporters and leaders.

Dignity Village in Portland, with a population of about seventy people, began as an encampment set up under a bridge in winter 2000, and sustained itself through several relocations and even mapped out its future in a document that treats everything from governance to resource management. By fall 2001, and after several moves, the city allowed Dignity to settle on a paved lot on the outskirts of town. By summer 2002, Dignity had registered as a nonprofit corporation. Visitors to its website can purchase signature items such as shirts and mugs; the organization has a building and physical-plan

FIGURE 22 The residents of Dignity Village in Portland, Oregon, design and build their own residences. The village's plan and the rules governing behavior are arrived at by consensus among the residents.

document, much of which is the work of activist architect Mark Lakeman.[24]

Dignity's ability to sustain itself is due primarily to the forcefulness of its leadership, particularly Lakeman. Its ongoing survival is also a result of Lakeman's understanding of the symbolic importance of design. Dignity includes a community space—a prominent structure among the ramshackle houses—that not only reinforces the sense of community within the village but also serves as a visual symbol for those on the outside. The visibility undoubtedly has helped the group politically, defining it not as a simple aggregation of homeless people but rather as a community with political proponents and advocates. Lakeman and other Dignity leaders felt that by creating such a village the participants are empowered to rebuild their own lives. But with stability come increasing complexities associated with cooperative settlement. The residents of Dignity have made rules, regulations, and even disputed their architect's vision, particularly over such priorities as form versus function.

Huts and tents are grouped into pods, each of which shares an open space and kitchen, that function as small neighborhoods; several such pods make up the village (figure 22). Each pod is deliberately kept small, reflecting the preferences of the residents for small groups composed of only a few individuals, a trait that MacDonald had postulated as characteristic of the street homeless. Though Dignity's population is an unusual one, the principle of its organization is not far different from conventional town planning.

FIGURE 23 The residences of the Domed Village in Los Angeles are easily assembled from manufactured panels. Are the distinctive residences a source of pride or do they stigmatize their residents?

The successes of Dignity Village notwithstanding, it is still a tough place. The paved site that the city makes available to the organizers has little drainage, and standing water is a common occurrence in the wet Oregon climate. Each dwelling is raised above the water on wood platforms, and walkways are formed of salvaged boards. And in spite of the residents' communal aspirations, there have been problems. Two huts have burned, making officials even more skeptical. Most residents of Dignity see it as transitional housing, and they leave when they are able. It remains to be seen whether a constantly changing group can sustain the enterprise, but those involved see it as a worthy experiment.

The leaders of Dignity Village point to Domed Village near downtown Los Angeles as their precedent. The conception of Domed Village began in the early 1990s when housing activist Ted Hayes teamed with the architect Craig Chamberlain, a manufacturer of Buckminster Fuller–type structures used for emergency and temporary dwellings. Hayes, a minister, became involved when he began to live among the homeless. After the city evicted a homeless encampment, he organized a nonprofit corporation with the goal of creating a legitimate and officially endorsed alternative. With the support of a real estate developer, who leased the property, and Arco Corporation, which provided financing for the project, Domed Village was constructed in late 1993 (figure 23).

One important difference between the two encampments is that the manufactured structures of Domed Village made the site instantaneously habitable; decisions about the site's organization and about the design of the dwellings themselves were not part of the process. Furthermore, much of Dignity Village's efforts were focused on seeking the endorsement of municipal authorities and obtaining operating funds. Government and business support, in contrast, has given Domed Village a presence very different from that of Dignity Village. The list of contributors to Domed Village reads like a *Who's Who* of Los Angeles, including corporations such as IBM and Disney as well as the U.S. Department of Housing and Urban Development, the Federal Emergency Management Agency, and even the California Highway Patrol.

Each dome sits on a concrete slab, and each is supplied with electricity and water (although the latter is limited to fire sprinklers required by the city). The domes themselves are assembled from curved, preformed fiberglass panels, each measuring several feet on a side. The edges of each panel have an integral flange that is bolted to the flange of another panel. Protrusions on some of the panels permit conventional doors and windows to be inserted in what is otherwise a rounded surface. The interior of the domes is divided in half to give privacy to families or individuals sharing the space. The dividing wall does not reach to the ceiling of the dome, as this would require a curving top, which is harder and more expensive to construct; this configuration has proved problematic, since sound from one side of the dome is projected into the other. The lack of insulation resulted in moisture collecting and dripping inside the domes when the interior temperature differed significantly from the temperature outside; each dome has now been retrofitted with taped-on interior insulation. The dwellings are spacious, light, and comfortable.

The villagers generally stay for two years (residence is limited to three years); many lavish attention on decorating the interior of their homes, and some even have elaborate stereos with surround-sound speakers, although televisions are prohibited (a television is available in the community dome). According to Hayes, a slender charismatic man with graying dreadlocks, the initial siting decision for the domes was partly a matter of expedience, but also of social engineering.[25] Hayes discerns a cause-and-effect relationship between social isolation and homelessness, and he maintains that overcoming homelessness requires interaction—even confrontation—with others. The architects originally considered incorporating bathrooms in each dome; the proposal was abandoned in favor of communal facilities clustered at some distance from the residences, in part to save money, but also to discourage the residents of the village from growing isolated. Hayes also believes that homelessness breeds a sort of narcissism. As Jeff, a two-year resident of the village puts it: "everything is about me, my space, mine, and I." To counter this attitude, residents must pay $70 per month, not as rent but as a gesture toward the community. The list of shared tasks includes such items as "clean dome edges, build a planter fence, garden, paint community sign, fix network log-on, and early child education." The spirit of Domed Village, which includes children among its residents, is that of a commune, not a homeless encampment, perhaps reflecting Hayes's background in radical movements of the 1960s. The village's population is limited to twenty-six residents, in part because of the size of the site and the limited resources available, but also as a deliberate choice. Hayes favors the construction of similar small villages rather than the expansion of Domed Village, but other Los Angeles homeless advocates have faulted the model as impractical—merely a drop in the lake of homelessness.

Dignity Village and Domed Village share two principal similarities. First, the residential structures of both are unusual, and their eccentricity is deliberate, directed in part toward fulfilling the needs of the residents but intended also as a form of public relations. In previous writings I have raised concerns about the appropriateness of deliberately making housing for low-income residents so evidently different from market-rate housing. Housing for the homeless walks a delicate line between stigma and pride: an unusual residence can be progressive or experimental, intended as a source of pride for those who inhabit it; but eccentricity also "marks" such structures as housing intended exclusively for the poor, and by implication, substandard. Should our building designs be experiments directed at a constituency that does not have the luxury of choice? At the same time, although the disparity of housing in the United States is deeply troubling, both Dignity Village and Domed Village seem to evoke pride among their inhabitants—pride in their physical structures as well as in the fact of having a place to live. Eccentric though they are, both are clearly preferable to life alone on the streets.

Second, the residents in these communities are self-governing, and their residency is accompanied by life-skills learning. There is an important link between inhabiting a physical space and the development of the person. When homeless people find a stable situation, they are in a better position to seek help for other problems that they encounter, and they are more likely to seek out contact with those who can help. Working and living with others are among the life skills made possible by these communities.

Present-day housing reformers are willing to design for nearly any lifestyle; their predecessors, in contrast, tied the form of housing to norms of socially acceptable behavior. The troubling question is whether these encampments or villages protect people from the hazards of being homeless, and by doing so encourage their residents to remain homeless. Shelters face a similar dilemma: does safety and comfort, beyond a certain level, encourage shelter residents to stay indefinitely? In sheltering the homeless are we perpetuating the situation and creating a permanent underclass, or truly helping those with the most acute needs? The leaders of both encampments address these issues by offering programs on-site and by limiting the duration of the residents' stay.

Most who work with the homeless feel these individuals must have opportunities to make contact with those who can assist them with aspects of homelessness beyond simply having a place to sleep. Solutions that include such forms of assistance are a more humane and life-affirming approach to homelessness than just letting people be and providing the means to do so, as with the City Sleeper.

SUPPORTIVE HOUSING

Supportive housing is any permanent housing that includes social services such as substance abuse programs, job training, or other health services. In the best cases the support services are on-site, and residents are encouraged, and often required by the terms of their lease, to participate in programs tailored to their needs.

Supportive housing is now widely accepted and, as we will see in the next chapter, has proved a cost-effective solution for people with special needs or who are at risk of homelessness. A national organization, the Corporation for Supportive Housing, was formed in 1991 to assist nonprofit developers and service providers in creating such projects. With eight offices in major metropolitan areas, the Corporation for Supportive Housing has invested $50 million, creating thousands of units throughout the country. Its goal, inspired by the National Alliance to End Homelessness, is to create 150,000 units of supportive housing within a decade for people with chronic illnesses or disabilities, low-income seniors, and single-parent families (among other constituencies).[26]

Supportive housing is not limited to a single type of structure (it might be an apartment, a house, or a collective dwelling), but much of the new urban supportive housing takes the form of buildings with housing situated above shops or public facilities. Placing shared facilities at the ground level provides a transition between the housing and the urban life beyond, which is precisely how the support facilities function. Conceptually the supportive service component is the buffer between a sanctuary—one's own dwelling—and the street, or the connection between the dwelling and the world beyond. Individuals who do not live in the housing, either because they have not graduated from transitional housing or because there are not enough supportive housing units available, use the facilities without encroaching on the private domain of the residents. This arrangement serves two purposes. First, it makes the supportive housing an integral part of the community. This is particularly important for those who have become estranged from social networks while homeless. Second, it creates a connection between those who have stable and permanent housing and those who do not.

The precedents for housing for the homeless and the very poor follow a general theme common in all housing: the more you have to spend, the greater the degree of privacy and the higher the level of amenities. The shelters had none, cubicles and lodging houses some, rooming houses more, and SROs a high degree of both. This level of designed independence and amenity is coincident with the degree of rules and management. In the absence of privacy and physical separation, rules are the substitute for what architecture has not accommodated. In some cases people are unable to tolerate the rules and choose a living situation ungoverned by such intrusions, often selecting life on the street.

At the beginning of this chapter, I noted that architecture reflects a society's values. While the homeless crisis can be seen as a failure of society, the evolution of the building types for the homeless is an indication that we, architects included, have looked in the mirror and did not like what we saw. In each of the housing situations described—shelters, flophouses, rooming houses, encampments, and now supportive housing—architects have played an important role. A new-found sense of social responsibility, not seen since the 1960s, has taken hold among many professionals. Those who sponsor this housing, both nonprofit service providers and government entities, understand the importance of design for those who inhabit the buildings and for those who live near them. Homelessness is a multifaceted problem, requiring the design of facilities with complex programs that must inspire the inhabitants and those who work with them. These designs are what architects can contribute to the solution.

SOME COSTS OF HOMELESSNESS 3

JUST AS THE SIZE of the United States' homeless population is difficult to calculate, assessing the economic and noneconomic costs of homelessness is a complex arithmetic. The direct economic costs include federal, state, and local government expenditures for housing, social services, public works, police and jails, food, and medical care. These government outlays are supplemented by private-sector expenditures by churches and other charitable institutions. In addition to money paid out, forgone economic opportunities enter into the costs of homelessness. Cities whose downtown streets are inhabited by homeless people, for example, forfeit sales tax and other revenue when homelessness leads to a decline in tourism or falling sales at local businesses.

The noneconomic costs of homelessness are both personal and social. Among communities, these include a degradation of the quality of life in public spaces where the homeless congregate. Among the newly homeless, the fiber of everyday life is entirely disrupted; dignity, choice, and ties to family and neighborhoods are lost. Those who remain homeless for long periods suffer a deterioration in mental and physical health, difficulties in finding and retaining employment, and a gradual alienation from everyday society. This chapter first looks at some of these costs, using San Francisco as an example. It concludes with a discussion of the cost of building housing for the homeless.

By far the largest share of costs for dealing with the homeless is borne by towns, cities, and counties. While other cities have a greater number of homeless, San Francisco, which is both a city and county, has the largest population of homeless people per capita of any city in the United States. Most of the federal government's allocation for homelessness goes directly to cities, and the overall federal contribution is small: $1.1 billion in fiscal 2002 (in contrast, the defense budget was approximately $350 billion). New York City spent $300 million on its shelter program in 2002, and this sum constitutes only a portion of the city's expenditures on the homeless. In 2001 San Francisco, a city one-tenth the size of New York, spent over $200 million on the homeless. This sum does not include the $100 million spent to acquire existing dwellings or to build new permanent affordable housing, or the $100 million general obligation bond passed by voters in 1996 to create new affordable housing.[1] Half the $200 million was spent on direct services to the homeless, including funds used to operate shelters, drug and alcohol rehabilitation programs, outreach, and other social programs, as well as a general assistance payout of up to $395 per individual per month. The other half went to city agencies that respond to the consequences of homelessness, including the police department, hospital emergency rooms, and sidewalk-cleaning units. By the city's count, San Francisco had a population of 7,100 homeless in October 2001; by simple division, then, the city spent $2,300 per homeless person per month. That sounds quite generous, equivalent to a month's rent for a very nice two-bedroom apartment in the city or a thirty-night stay in an inexpensive hotel (or, double occupancy, at a good hotel). When local reporters and politicians did the math, they were outraged at the sums. But simple division fails to take the pattern of expenditures into account. When a homeless person is admitted to a hospital, the cost is approximately $450 a night, or $3,150 a week. Thus while the sickest of the homeless received thousands of dollars of needed medical care, other homeless people received less than $400 a month in assistance. A good portion of the money that the city spends "on the homeless," moreover, goes to cleaning up after street-dwellers, not to finding them a place to live.

The cost of keeping someone in a residence is far less than the cost of returning him or her to one. Once a person becomes homeless, the "homeless system" is activated, and with it the cost of services, shelter, and emergency assistance. The cost of an affordable, subsidized dwelling in New York is $700 per month, or $23 per day; the cost of accommodating a family in a shelter is $100 per day.[2] By the mid-1990s, the national average cost of a bed in an emergency shelter was over $8,000 per year, more than the payout of federal housing subsidies under Section 8 of the Federal Housing Act, administered by the Department of Housing and Urban Development (HUD), which subsidizes the difference between market rents and what qualifying low-income families can afford to pay.[3]

DEALING WITH DIRT

In a survey conducted during the summer of 2002, San Franciscans ranked homelessness as their city's most pressing problem—above crime, housing costs, and unemployment.[4] The San Francisco Convention and Visitor's Bureau mounted a $50,000 billboard campaign imploring officials to clean up the streets, arguing that mean, dirty streets threatened tourism and convention business;[5] in response, the city's board of supervisors passed a law banning public urination and defecation. The gesture, though understandable, ignores the simple facts of life: What facilities are people living on the street supposed to use? What economic or enforcement interest is served in fining a person who is destitute? Is it the best use of police officers' time to have them ticketing homeless people for public urination? Having to use the street is humiliating, and using the street as a public toilet is sometimes a statement of despair, anger, and defiance. As one homeless man put it: "After all the hassles I go through out on the street, you gonna tell me I can't do the most basic things a man has to do—where I want and when I want?"[6]

Several years ago, recognizing that tourists and residents also needed public facilities, the city purchased and installed some twenty sophisticated coin-operated, self-cleaning public bathrooms. Twenty-five cents buys twenty minutes in one of these $200,000 French-designed devices. The toilets have been effective in certain areas of the city, but some are used by addicts and prostitutes; others malfunction and sit idle, awaiting repair. As a result, many neighborhoods have barred the city from installing them. One local minister suggested that the city hire homeless people to monitor activity and summon police when necessary (perhaps by analogy with bathroom attendants, which are common in Europe and not limited to fancy hotels or restaurants); the proposal was ignored.

To clean street defecation, San Francisco acquired seventeen heavy-duty sidewalk-scouring devices, known as Green Machines, at a cost of about $25,000 each. The Green Machines can clean only horizontal surfaces, however, and some defiant homeless people have responded by positioning themselves so that their waste is smeared on storefront windows; the machines cannot keep up with the mess. A few storeowners have granted the homeless permission to sleep in their stores' entryways in exchange for serving as nighttime "guards." The guards are given a bucket to use as a chamber pot, and they clean their buckets every morning. But most storeowners use gates to close off their storefronts. Downtown streets that were once a lively mixture of display windows and elegant entryways have become a continuous line of metal at night.

In addition to purchasing the Green Machines, San Francisco spent over $650,000 in 2001 to deal with almost a thousand shopping carts left unattended in public places.[7] Contaminated needles pose the greatest threat to the city workers assigned to this task, but under the blankets and clothes they also find feces, rats, and lice. For the general public, the carts are noisy eyesores and health hazards; for the stores that own the carts, the loss of their use and the cost of reclaiming and decontaminating them are an added expense. For the homeless, however, shopping carts serve as closets, dresser drawers, linen closets, and cupboards, as well as purses, briefcases, or backpacks. The carts are convenient, available, and mobile spaces for the short-term and long-term storage of clothing, bedding, utensils, photographs, and memorabilia—indeed, everything that they own, unless they have left items with friends or are among the few who band together to rent a storage locker. Because homeless people have so little, they are fiercely protective of what they do have. In recognition of that fact, city workers carefully remove and inventory the items when they confiscate the carts; the items are stored for ninety days, during which their owners may reclaim their property. This system was instituted after some homeless people accused city workers of stealing their belongings. Local attorneys, working pro bono, filed suit on behalf of the complainants. One homeless man accepted a $2,950 settlement for the loss of two Persian rugs and a laptop computer that he claimed had been in his cart when it was seized.[8] For the city, settling the case was less expensive than going to court, and the new inventory system is less expensive than settling a spate of lawsuits. But the $650,000 per year that the city spends on confiscating carts and processing their contents do nothing to reduce the number of homeless in the city. That same $650,000 could cover the cost of building ten units of transitional housing.

The carts are but one instance in which the

needs of homeless people—here, the need to transport and protect their meager belongings—conflict with the desires of the general public, which expects clean, unobstructed sidewalks. Putting aside the fact that the carts are stolen, both sides have legitimate claims. What might seem a simple issue—getting the carts off the streets—has complex public health, political, and legal implications.

LOSS OF USE

Public spaces—streets, sidewalks, plazas, and squares—are intended to be used by all. But in many cities residents have in effect ceded portions of various public spaces to the homeless. Nonhomeless people do not enter these spaces unless they must, and then they walk through them at a quick clip. Rousting homeless people from public spaces during the day is problematic; since the homeless have nowhere to go, rousting them simply puts them somewhere else. New York City mayor Rudolph Giuliani was credited with cleaning up Manhattan in the 1990s, and indeed, there were far fewer homeless to be seen on the upscale shopping streets and near the corporate headquarters; they were sent to the outer boroughs, where most of the new shelters were built.

Nonetheless, all citizens have a right to be in a public space during its hours of operation as long as they adhere to certain basic norms of behavior, even if their presence makes others uncomfortable. The conflict between the desires of the general public and those of the homeless has become particularly pointed in some public libraries.

Among the most ingenious features of San Francisco's urban design are the alleys that run between major streets. Intended as service roads, they also provide light and ventilation for offices and stores that extend from the main street to the alley. In many of these alleys, groups of homeless reside among the dumpsters and parked cars; some use the alleys for sleeping, others treat them as bathrooms. The stench is sometimes so overpowering that people in the adjacent buildings never open the windows that face the alley. For some, this loss of use has an additional cost: deprived of natural ventilation, they use more air conditioning.

Union Square, situated in the heart of San Francisco's upscale shopping district, reopened in 2002 after a $25 million redesign. The square needed an upgrade, but one of the principal factors in the selection of the new design was to make the space less attractive for homeless people and to make their presence easier to monitor. The old Union Square had hedges and benches that were not visible from the street; forty years ago, the square was a haven for men living in nearby residential hotels, who would spend much of the day sitting on the benches, reading (figure 24). By the 1980s, however, these men were replaced by the homeless, who would lie unseen among the hedges. Shoppers walked along the perimeter of the square, rather than through the plaza, to avoid the homeless. The new, open design (figure 25) is more inviting for shoppers and tourists; it is very deliberately not a welcoming place for the homeless. Although the redesign of Union Square, like the redesign of other public areas, such as Bryant Park in New York City, reclaims a highly visible public space, merely dispersing the homeless does nothing to solve their problems.

What price we are willing to pay to make the homeless less visible? Are we willing to pay the costs for stricter enforcement of vagrancy laws? And if we are, are we then willing to build more jails for the scofflaws? If we spend less on critical care for the homeless, could we devote more resources and provide more attention to others with medical needs? Or would the money that we are tempted to spend on removing vagrants from our

FIGURE 24 Union Square in San Francisco in the 1960s. Men living in nearby residential hotels often spent their days sitting in the square.

FIGURE 25 Union Square today. The redesign opens up the space, making sitting areas clearly visible from surrounding streets.

view be better spent providing them with transitional and permanent housing?

HOW SHOULD WE SPEND MONEY ON HOMELESSNESS?

Most would agree that the money being spent on remedying the impact of the homeless on the urban environment does little to reduce homelessness. If we could set aside some of that money, how might it be better spent? Simply building housing does not address the situation of low-income individuals who need job services, nor of those who are ill and need mental health and medical services, nor of single mothers with young children who need child care. Social services will continue to be a necessary component of assisting the homeless, but the homeless, by definition, need a place to live.

The most cost-effective means of combating homelessness is to prevent the loss of a home. Offering low-interest loans or housing subsidies and curtailing evictions are less expensive than building new facilities. Yet creating new housing for those who become homeless is also part of the solution. The continuum of care, of which services are a vital element, also comprises shelters, supportive housing (perhaps in single room occupancy hotels [SROs]), and other types of independent permanent housing. In each instance, thoughtful architecture is a necessary component of the solution: if the places we build do not meet the needs of the residents and those who work with them, and if the facilities and those who occupy them are rejected by their communities, the expenditures will have been wasted.

WHAT DOES HOUSING COST?

Construction constitutes a smaller portion of the overall cost of a building than one might think: land purchase, financing, and "soft" costs are higher than bricks and sticks. Here's a simple example. Jo buys a piece of land for $100,000 and intends to build a two-thousand-square-foot, three-bedroom house on it. She hires an architect (a good thing to do) and a contractor. The overall cost for the contractor is $150 per square foot, or $300,000. Of that, approximately 15 percent, or $45,000, represents the contractor's overhead, so the construction component is around $255,000. The architect, engineer, building permit, and other nonconstruction costs add at least another 20 percent of the $300,000 (that is, $60,000) to the total. The overall cost of Jo's house will be a little over $460,000. She will likely finance as much as 75 to 80 percent of that amount. Payments on a thirty-year mortgage will cost her about $2,000 per month for 360 months. At the end of that time she owns her home (which presumably is worth much more than it cost), but she will have paid nearly $720,000 on the mortgage; she thus likely paid $500,000 more than the cost of the actual construction ($255,000), which is only around 30 percent of the total.

The overall costs unrelated to construction increase as the size and scope of the project increase. The soft costs of new shelters like those discussed in the previous chapter will be several million dollars; these include costs not usually associated with building a house, such as an environmental impact report, public hearings, and special building inspections by the health department and the department of social welfare.

REDUCING COSTS

Many have posited that moving much of the work from the site and into a factory would reduce the cost of building housing. Certainly reducing the extent of on-site construction and standardizing

FIGURE 26 Mobile homes are less expensive than construction housing, but their single story limits their use to low-density areas. A few have attempted to overcome this inherent limitation, as in this 1960s demonstration (SkyeRise Terrace by the Frey Building Company), by placing the units onto a concrete support structure.

the product give builders more control over material and labor costs, and work can continue regardless of the weather. The quality of manufactured housing (known colloquially as mobile homes) has improved over time, and the industry continues to provide single-family housing at a cost far lower than that of housing constructed on-site. Nonetheless, there are limits on the economies obtainable through manufactured housing.

Manufactured homes, because of their structure and the materials used in their manufacture, are generally limited to a single story, so a large expanse of land is required in order to place an economically feasible number of units on a site; few such sites are available within or near cities that are close to jobs, transportation, and social services. One could create a factory-produced module that achieves higher density, but doing so would obviate the cost-efficiency of housing manufactured within a factory. Such a module requires either a separate independent structure onto which dwelling-sized modules can be placed (figure 26) or stronger walls to support additional modules (figure 27). It also requires variation in the overall product in order to take necessary advantage of diverse site configurations and contexts.

Factory-produced low-cost housing has not been widely adopted in the United States, yet many continue to proffer this as a solution for the homeless. San Francisco builder Jim Reid has created a small, fully equipped dwelling (figures 28 and 29) modeled on the emergency cottages set up in San Francisco's parks after the 1906 earthquake (figure 30). Reid sees his 300-square-foot mini-houses as an option for housing the homeless, but their costs (estimated by Reid at $50,000 per unit, including land purchase and infrastructure) approach those of higher-density conventional buildings; Reid himself acknowledges that only a few should be set up in one place.[9] Dennis Davey has designed similarly small-scale houses (called "Hom4Me") that take their inspiration from mountain cabins rather than from the Victorian cottages of Reid's design. With a floor area of 225

FIGURE 27 Each module of Habitat in Montreal supports several others. The structure needed to support these modules makes the Habitat model more costly than other forms of manufactured housing.

square feet, Davey's cabins are constructed of prefabricated panels and can be assembled in three days at a unit cost of $13,000.[10] These low-rise, low-density houses are a useful option where space is available, but they are not a feasible solution in cities, where the cost of land is generally high, and the low density does little to satisfy the housing need.

Acknowledging the limitations of manufacturing entire dwellings, some builders manufacture elements of buildings in factories, for subsequent assembly on-site. At the Bishop Francis A. Quinn Cottages in Sacramento (designed by the late Brent Smith for Mercy Housing), each resident has a narrow, one-bedroom cottage that was partially constructed off-site and assembled on permanent foundations. A cottage of 375 square feet costs approximately $60,000—as much as a unit built entirely on-site. Because each is a separate dwelling and no walls are shared, and because a site can accommodate only a small number of units, this method of housing construction results in little cost savings. Furthermore, the dwellings are too small to serve other functions, so this modest complex of sixty single-story units includes a separate community building (where classes, group meals, and social service are provided), thereby increasing development costs.[11]

FIGURE 28 Jim Reid's small self-contained houses are modeled on cottages built as temporary accommodation for those left homeless by the 1906 San Francisco earthquake.

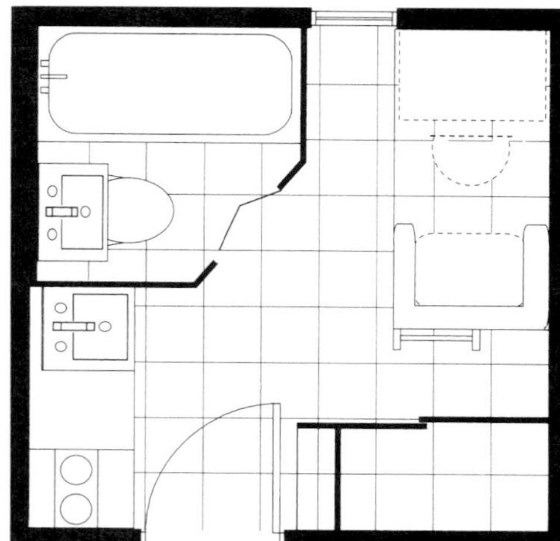

FIGURE 29 Plan of one of Jim Reid's houses, proposed as permanent accommodation for the homeless in San Francisco.

Walls that must accommodate manufactured windows, doors, electrical outlets, or finishes require skilled installers, and each piece must be designed for a specific position in the building. The less variation, the lower the cost, but the specificity of the program, site, and size often militates against repetition. Regulatory and political constraints also make factory production problematic. If major components are manufactured, perhaps in another jurisdiction, who is responsible for their inspection? A project required to use union workers, as many government-funded buildings are, would presuppose a unionized factory. These issues also limit the economic advantages of the product.

Finally, one of the most important obstacles to factory production is the nature of the homebuilding industry in the United States. Large builders focus primarily on high-end, single-family developments, but the industry is in fact composed largely of small independent contractors, each minimally capitalized. These builders rely on a floating labor force and on subcontractors to perform specific tasks, such as mechanical and electrical work. Contracting is primarily a construc-

FIGURE 30 Earthquake cottages in San Francisco, ca. 1906. Hundreds of these small dwellings housed those who lost homes in the San Francisco earthquake and fire. Some were later moved to other sites and remain in use today.

tion management enterprise. Most contractors have few regular employees, and they generally do not own the heavy equipment required to lift and install room-sized modules; rather, they work with small building components such as wood studs and beams, lightweight premanufactured trusses, or bricks, which can be handled by a few people and less-expensive equipment.

The factory system presupposes a repetitive product and a large, guaranteed market. The product must therefore appeal to a wide variety of buyers, be acceptable in many communities, transportable over long distances (at a reasonable cost) to reach its market, and be adaptable to different site conditions. These characteristics hold true for cars and refrigerators but not for housing, and particularly not the kind of housing that the homeless need. Shifting construction to factories would reduce costs by only a modest amount, and the savings would be limited to the enclosing structure, which constitutes less than a third of construction costs. Factory production might reduce these costs by 10 percent. In Jo's house, with its "hard" construction cost of $255,000, that would amount to $7,600, or a little more than 1 percent of the $720,000 overall cost of the project.

The character of the construction industry is reflected in its products and equipment: power nail-guns, manufactured windows, bathtubs with integral wall panels that do not require tiling, and sheets of material such as plywood that are easily acquired and handled by a few workers; such products can even be found at the increasing number of consumer-oriented do-it-yourself outlets. In spite of its decentralized nature, the building industry is highly integrated. Lumber, nails, and other building components are standardized and universally accessible. Each component is small, not merely so that it can be handled easily but also to permit flexibility in assembly. All types and configurations of building are possible within this system, so that local building codes and regional preferences can be accommodated.

Still, there are ways to reduce the cost of buildings even within this seemingly infinite choice of components. Repetition saves money; if we design buildings that use a recurrent structural span—the space from wall to wall—then each spanning member can be cut to the same length, saving time and materials and reducing the risk of construction error. Contractors love this consistency, and they reflect this preference in their prices. Similarly, if we build a multi-unit building with identical kitchens and bathrooms throughout, then the cost of cabinets, appliances, plumbing, and electrical work will be reduced. If this is a multistory building, and each of these units stacks directly above the other, there is even more efficiency.[12]

If we construct several identical buildings, better still. Materials, appliances, doors, windows, and precut lumber can be stockpiled. This is how the rapidly growing extended-stay hotel industry works. Its buildings are essentially SROs with individual units, each with a kitchen and bathroom. Their owners or financers find sites that can accommodate the plan of each basic building, requiring few design variations. As a result, a studio unit costs approximately $43,000 to build, one-third less than a comparable unit in a site-specific urban SRO.[13]

This approach to construction, however, does not lend itself to building housing for the homeless. First, it would take a nationally organized effort to ensure that these economies are realized. The needs of diverse populations in cities throughout the United States would have to be satisfied by a single prototype building, but homeless populations are not identical, and such a centralized, organized, and capitalized effort is not feasible to the same extent that it is for the hotel industry. Housing for the homeless, moreover, must meet local needs and regulations; it depends heavily on local funding and operates within the context of local programs; and it must be accepted by the community. Although guidelines can ensure that what gets built meets programmatic needs, the buildings themselves are nonetheless unique to their sites.

Universities have discovered this reality. University housing, directed largely toward a constituency of unmarried students without dependents, comprises a limited number of forms similar to the types of housing we might build for the homeless: dormitories with shared bathroom and dining facilities, suites, or SROs. Dormitories are to some extent similar to transitional shelters or boardinghouses, suites resemble apartments with on-site program spaces, and SROs are essentially the same as the supportive housing model. But the per-bed cost of university housing construction is very expensive—often twice the cost of comparable models for the homeless. At the University of California, Berkeley, for example, building a new dormitory cost nearly $80,000 per bed, while a new transitional housing project in nearby Marin County with many similar features cost $40,000 per bed.[14] The difference between the materials (and type of construction) conventionally used for dormitories and transitional housing—respectively, concrete frame and wood—accounts for only 3 percent of the difference in their costs. Nearly 10 percent of the university's higher cost is the result of the institution's oversight apparatus—more bureaucracy—and self-imposed requirements; the latter include adherence to the university's urban design and planning guidelines, which reflect both community pressure and institutional expectations. Another major difference is the overall building efficiency—the ratio between usable (assignable) space and the overall (gross) built space. University buildings, such as Berkeley's dormitory, typically occupy a limited space, which obligates these institutions to construct tall buildings. Taller buildings need additional space for stairways, elevators, hallways, and a heavier frame to support this added weight, all of which reduce efficiency. The actual living space in Berkeley's new dormitory constitutes only 62 percent of the building. Although the pattern of dormitories on urban university campuses is not unique, the buildings themselves, defined by their setting, are.

Other forms of institutional housing, however, are more cost-efficient. Minimum-security prisons can be built at a low cost per bed—the state of Oregon built several such facilities during the 1990s for as little as $22,000 per bed[15]—and they have several structural features in common with emergency shelters: large sleeping wards, classrooms, exercise spaces, and dining halls. But minimum-security prisons are built on large tracts of flat land, and they usually comprise a single floor with few hallways; most are based on a replicable prototype. The buildings are stand-alone and do not need community approval, as would a housing project for the homeless within an urban neighborhood.

In the absence of feasible models for reducing the costs of building housing for the homeless, another approach is to reduce the quality of the materials. Compromising on the quality of the materials used in construction, however, offers few cost savings. The main difference between expensive housing and modest housing is in the quality (and cost) of finishes—cabinets, windows, lighting, countertops, and floors. The principal structural elements—walls, roofs, and foundations—are uniform, and construction techniques and building codes apply equally to supportive housing for the homeless and a luxury condominium. Furthermore, if we consider the long-term cost of housing, including maintenance and repair, there is little to be gained by trying to do it with low-quality materials.

HOUSING TYPE AND COST

Some types of housing are inherently more expensive than others on a square-foot basis. The larger the dwelling, the lower the unit cost. If we are creating supportive housing for homeless single adults and the program calls for individual studio units, then each will have a small kitchen and a bathroom—the most expensive elements in a dwelling. A building comprising a hundred units will require a hundred kitchens and bathrooms: each unit might have a floor space of only 500 square feet, but the cost of these expensive components must be accounted for in this small area, driving up the overall cost. On the other hand, building a hundred two-bedroom apartments of 800 square feet each still requires the same hundred kitchens and bathrooms. The square-foot cost of the studios will be higher than the two-bedroom apartments, although the net cost will be lower since the building is smaller.

Why is this an issue? Building costs are often calculated in dollars per square foot. This measure is a convenient means of establishing an overall budget before construction begins, since it establishes a unit cost for a program that defines how much space is needed. Sometimes building costs are expressed as a cost per bed, in order to relate construction costs to the number of people served. In the example above, the cost per bed of studio units will also be higher than that of two-bedroom apartments. The assumption is that the studio will house one person while the apartment will house three or four (one or two adults and two children).

Developers of housing for the homeless (as well as the facilities' neighbors) often prefer to limit the number of residents and the size of the building. A smaller project is easier to manage, better adapted to delivering social services, and perceived to have less impact on the community. But the smaller the project, the higher the unit cost, whatever the measure. Staging construction—getting the equipment and laborers on the site—creates a considerable initial expense, but the relative initial cost decreases with a larger building. The first square foot of construction is much more expensive than the last. If the overall building project is small, economies of scale cannot be realized. Small may be beautiful, but it is also costly.

Given these measures, individual studios for homeless adults are costlier than most other types of housing, whereas the costs of housing for homeless families will be comparable to conventional apartments. Supportive housing with services onsite incurs additional costs for the nonhousing space. Budget constraints thus often result in buildings that place the homeless in collective living situations in which elements such as kitchens, bathrooms, and even bedrooms are shared. In most instances, moreover, this form of housing is not well suited to the population it is intended to serve.

Housing for the homeless has one other economic obstacle. Sites for such use are usually not prime land (otherwise a developer would have snatched them up long before), and they often come burdened with features that increase costs. The best sites on which to build economically are rectangular and flat, with good soil that has no traces of toxic chemicals (the cleanup of which imposes substantial costs on the owner or operator). In an ideal world, neighbors accept building on the land, and the site is unencumbered by other regulatory obstacles such a historic designation. But such an ideal group of circumstances is rare, and rarer still when building affordable housing or housing for the homeless. More often, affordable sites are burdened with major technical or political problems. Even if a site is available at no cost (perhaps donated or underwritten through a redevelopment agency), considerable expenses will likely be incurred in developing it for use. Those who build the housing have little flexibility: the facilities must be situated where there are homeless, where there are services that homeless need, and where the zoning regulations allow the facilities to be built.

SO WHAT SHOULD WE DO?

First, we have to accept that there is no such thing as affordable housing. Building is building, and a wood stud costs the same whether placed in a luxury condominium or in housing for the homeless. The building codes are identical, as are the methods of construction. Of course, a market-rate dwelling is likely to be larger, but floor area is a minor issue in overall cost. The quality of the finishes will be better as well in a market-rate dwelling, but we still need high-quality construction if housing for the homeless is to be sustainable and acceptable in communities.

In fact, subsidized housing is often more expensive to produce than market-rate housing. The reasons why this is so include the physical configuration of sites typically available for subsidized housing, the need to use high-quality construction to ensure that the housing will fit into communities and not deteriorate, and the generally modest

FIGURE 31 Bay windows are a relatively inexpensive means of enlivening facades and bringing light into dwellings.

size of most subsidized housing projects. This does not mean that we should ignore ways to keep costs down. The challenge is to build as efficiently as possible while meeting the programmatic intent: to provide dignified places in which to live.

Variety within Uniformity

Some uniformity is necessary to keep costs down. There is little benefit, for example, in building an SRO with fifty unique units. The building may comprise two or three different unit types, perhaps reflecting different occupant profiles (single adults, families, or disabled occupants). The site configuration may preclude replication of a single unit throughout the building: an L-shaped site, for example, would result in an inside-corner unit that is by necessity different in configuration from those along the length of the L. But even with three unit types, there is little reason to make each bathroom and kitchen unique.

A simple building can be architecturally interesting. Units placed on the corners can be slightly modified to take advantage of the opportunity for another window. Minor variations in the plan enliven the exterior, providing visual diversity while creating special spaces within. The bay window is an obvious example. A bay protruding from the facade of the building is an extension of the human activity within—a recognition of the individual unit within a larger complex (figure 31). From the interior, the bay can be a source of additional daylight, an extension to a room, or a reading or eating nook.

Varying the disposition of the units within a ba-

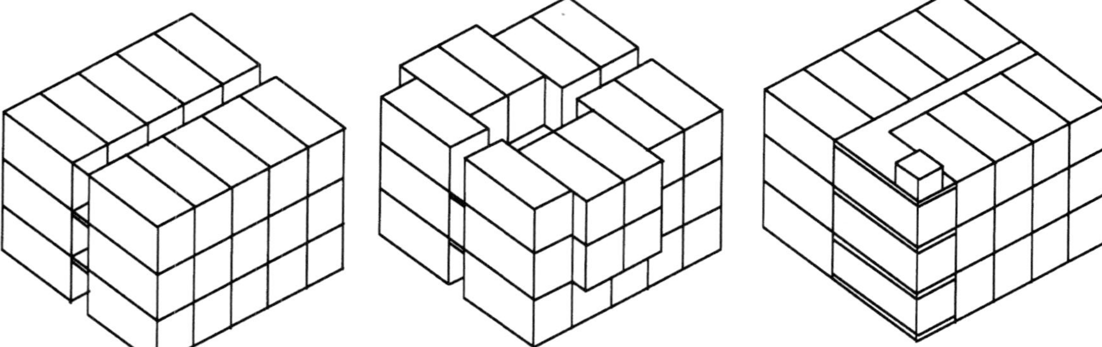

FIGURE 32 Variety is possible even in repetitive units. The simple double-loaded corridor building (left) is relieved both inside and out by a slightly projecting unit (center). Placing public rooms on the corner (right) creates a distinctive entry for the building and provides a common space for each floor's residents.

sic plan can provide visual interest, both at the building's exterior and in the interior usable space, at minimal cost (figure 32). Removing a single unit at the end of a corridor of aligned units brings light into the corridor and creates a common space that is usable by all the occupants. This common space might be differentiated from the dwellings by a distinct window, indicating that there are large and small, public and private spaces within. In a multistory building, this stack of common rooms can become a separate architectural form, placed at a prominent corner that signals the entry to the building. Simply shifting some dwellings outward so that they project from the building's facade creates a larger area along the corridor and enlivens an otherwise uniform plane. The interior space might be a vestibule at the entry to several units, facilitating chance meetings and a sense of community.

These design strategies cost more than a simple box, but they maintain the essential repetition of the units and the overall structure, while yielding significant architectural gains.

Creative Use of What You Already Have

All buildings have walls, roofs, windows, and doors, and architects make hundreds of choices for each element. A wall has color, texture, and thickness, and it may be punctuated with doors and windows. A window has a size and shape, as well as a frame (sometimes differentiated by color), a method of opening (sliding, double-hung, or casement), and a specific placement in the wall. The cumulative effect of these decisions is what gives a building its architectural character. Affordable-housing architects are particularly adept at using the basic elements of a building to create distinctive forms. Varying the color of a window's frame, in conjunction with diverse window placements, can create a larger pattern, giving the building an elegance that belies its modest budget and use. Treating various lengths of a building differently can make large buildings seem as if they comprise a set of smaller structures.

Elements attached to the building can also be creatively manipulated (figure 33). Rain must be

FIGURE 33 Roof overhangs, color variations, diverse windows, awnings, and vine-covered trellises add diversity to a simple structure at little additional cost.

directed away from buildings by gutters and downspouts, but these elements can be decorative as well as functional. So too can window awnings, which reduce energy costs while brightening the facade. Courtyards often have walls and trellises that define the building's territory and improve security, while creating shade and shadows that bring elements of the building into relief during the course of the day. Roofs as well provide opportunities for innovative design. Even simple flat roofs can be varied by raising some areas above others or by using cornices. Sloping roofs can be hipped or gabled, and they can have overhangs, dormers, and intersecting shapes.

None of these elements are mere decoration. Each has a function and must be included in the building, but the incremental cost of using these elements effectively and creatively is negligible and the benefits great. Making housing special is the value that architects add. A building that residents can be proud of and enjoy living in, and that the community welcomes, does not have to be more expensive than the alternative.

Spending Where It Counts

Another strategy to achieve the best architecture at the lowest cost is to increase the budget for a few selected elements. To make this expenditure feasible, the other parts of the building are designed as efficiently as possible, perhaps by limiting the number of bays, or the variations on the facades. Architects often use this approach in designing shelters and transitional housing. The main functional elements of the building—sleeping areas, bathrooms, dining halls—are straightforward, but some special place, such as the chapel, is given architectural prominence. These components do not necessarily have to be buildings. Courtyards, for example, while adding to a project's cost, can serve several important functions in housing for the homeless, such as providing protected play areas for children or a community garden. The exterior walls of a building are expensive elements, since they require windows, waterproofing, a finished interior surface, insulation, and electrical wiring. A simple box encloses the greatest amount of interior space with the least amount of exterior wall, and it contains the least amount of foundation and roof for the area enclosed. A hole in that box increases the extent of the building's exterior wall, the length of its foundation, and the amount of roof. When the elements have programmatic importance, however—as a courtyard can in providing a secure common area—the added costs may be a worthy investment.

Big, But Not Too Big

Determining the size of a facility, be it a shelter, a supportive housing SRO, or apartments, requires planners to balance the need to accommodate as large a population as possible, while ensuring each individual's access to services, within economic and social constraints. On the one hand, a facility that can accommodate a larger number of people reduces the number of homeless. The more services provided by the facility, the more efficient its operation. Larger buildings, as we have seen, create economies of scale. On the other hand, most service providers and nonprofit developers do not have access to the level of funding that is required for large projects. Although the square-foot or per-bed costs decrease as the building area increases, larger buildings cost more, and that cost may exceed available funds.

Furthermore, communities tend to oppose the construction of very large facilities; smaller buildings that fit discreetly into communities raise fewer objections. Most who develop and operate these projects, moreover, prefer smaller facilities, which are more easily managed and often better suited to their residents. A sense of community and personal contact are more easily achieved in a fifty-unit building than in a two-hundred-unit building.

Above a certain point, larger multistory buildings require a more costly infrastructure and additional fire protection systems, as well as more elevators and additional support spaces, than do small buildings. A wood-framed structure is limited to four floors (building the ground floor in concrete raises the total to five). Costs rise considerably, however, when buildings are not framed in wood, and fewer qualified contractors are available to build these projects, making the bidding less competitive. On the other hand, building too small is not cost-effective. A small project will require the same amount of effort by the architect and the developer as a large one. Small projects will be more expensive on a per-bed basis.

The goal, then, is to balance housing as many people as possible with political and economic viability. The number of units will depend on the site, the local politics, the capacity of the service provider or developer, and the availability of funding. Most supportive housing projects comprise approximately fifty units. Shelter operators prefer to limit capacity to forty beds, but they acknowledge that this is not efficient.

Lower the Soft Costs

In 2002, I sent a homeless housing project that I had designed out to contractors for bids. Much of the project was publicly funded. As a consequence, contractors, in addition to offering formal bids for the project, were required to complete several forms attesting to their ability to meet the city's goals for participation by minority- and women-owned businesses in the construction. In addition, the low bidder, which by law we were compelled to accept, was required to prepare regular statements certifying that those who worked on the project in particular jobs were being paid the prevailing wage for those tasks.

These requirements, common in many cities, have worthy objectives, but their effect is to increase a project's cost. First, many contractors who had worked with me on other similar projects without such rules declined to bid on this project: they simply lacked the financial or office staff to manage the paperwork. One contractor had provided preliminary cost estimates indicating an amount far below the lowest bid, but found the prospect of compliance paperwork too onerous and declined to submit a formal bid. When the financial bids were opened, the lowest bidder's price was 10 percent less than the others; he had met the goals for city minority participation, was willing to undertake the paperwork requirements, but had filled out some of the forms incorrectly. We were compelled as a consequence to reject his bid. Ultimately the project costs exceeded the winning bid by 10 percent, a difference that had to be raised privately.

The project delivery system, which includes the selection of the architects and the contractors, is more cumbersome for publicly funded construction projects than for projects that are privately funded. The requirement that contractors must pay the prevailing wage, equivalent to union wages, can add as much as 15 percent to the construction component—a difference that far exceeds cost savings effected by strategies to reduce the cost of building. The competitive bidding of projects, a seemingly logical way to reduce costs, often has the opposite effect. The lowest bidder, although fully licensed, may not be the one best suited to the project, often resulting in errors and delays. In privately funded projects, a contractor may be selected early in the process, perhaps at the same time as the architect, and then the construction price negotiated. The contractor selection is based on several measures, including the ability to manage cost. This system allows the contractor and architect to work collaboratively during design, choosing the best methods and most suitable materials for the construction. Some contractors or suppliers may be willing to lower their prices because they are sympathetic to the goals of the project, but only if they are not required to submit a competitive bid and manage the city-required human resources documentation, both of which are time-consuming.

City bureaucracies can affect cost in the selection of an architect. A service provider may wish to retain architects with whom they have had a good working relationship from a previous project. Their knowledge of the client and program might expedite the design and ultimately its costs. The provider alone does not make the selection: the city funding department will also be involved. The favored architects are but one firm among several considered, and their selection is not guaranteed. Bureaucracies are rarely flexible, nor do they often allow for the exercise of reasonable judgment. They are not able to adjust rules to mediate between equally worthy social and political objectives—the assurance of a union wage and participation of women and minorities in construction projects—against the social objective of helping the homeless.

All housing construction entails administrative costs. These include the developer's management costs, building permits and inspection fees, and architect and engineering fees. Some organizations or institutions, such as universities, have very high soft costs. Nonprofit and market-rate housing developers alike incur costs associated with obtaining entitlements and funding. Like the building itself, larger developers are advantaged by economies of scale, since they have more project managers and administrative support for construction. On the other hand, they must continuously build—and build large—to justify this overhead. The smaller the organization and the less reliant it is on public funding, the lower its administrative costs. But smaller nonprofit developers and service providers can manage only modest projects—and only a few at a time. Nonprofit organizations such as the Corporation for Supportive Housing and the Local Initiative Support Corporation provide assistance to those developing housing for the homeless, thereby shouldering some of the burden. Some community-minded financial institutions, such as Union Bank of California, provide grants to assist nascent nonprofit developers through their community development projects.[16]

Donors want some assurances that the money they give to charity will go to those in need and not to supporting the inefficiencies of the soft costs that accompany the public money, even if it is only a small portion of the overall funding. The same holds true for building housing for the homeless. The goal is to use most of the funds for the actual construction. A project that is wholly privately funded, with fewer restrictions and lower overheads, is more efficient than publicly funded housing, but the private sector alone cannot meet the demand. Some government funding, perhaps diverted from environmental cleanup costs, will be necessary if we are to build enough housing for the current population, recognizing that with it come the expenses of regulation and management.

THE SERVICE-HOUSING COST RELATIONSHIP

A study recently undertaken by the University of Pennsylvania sought to determine whether placing homeless individuals with severe mental illnesses in supportive housing reduced the cost of services. The study compared the relative costs of mental health services for housed and homeless individuals, factoring in the cost of housing. It concluded:

> homeless people placed in supportive housing experience marked reductions in shelter use, hospitalizations (regardless of type), length of stay per hospitalization, and time incarcerated. Prior to placement in housing, homeless people with severe mental illness used an average of $40,449 per person per year in such services (in 1999 dollars). Placement in housing through the New York/New York program (NY/NY) was associated with a reduction in service use of $16,282 per housing unit per year, adjusting for concurrent changes in the controls' service use patterns. Unit costs per year for the supportive housing are estimated at $17,277, which would result in a modest cost of $995 per unit per year over the first two years of placement. Overall, the NY/NY initiative, which included some licensed community mental health residences as well, resulted in a net cost of $1,908 per unit per year, or $6.9 million.[17]

The authors are careful to point out factors that might have skewed the results, such as the possibility that the test group used mental health services more extensively in preparation for moving to permanent housing than it otherwise would have, but they maintain that the study's conclusions still hold: the group in supportive housing required fewer mental health services. One reason advanced for this result is that the resolution of their housing crisis enabled these individuals to cope with other issues, reducing both the need for and the duration of inpatient hospital care. (The study did not address whether other types of services typically used by the homeless, such as emergency food programs, might also be reduced by accommodation in supportive housing.) But it is likely that the costs of homelessness discussed at the beginning of this chapter, such as public works expenditures for dealing with shopping carts and street cleaning, court costs, and police-related expenses for crime victims, would be similarly reduced. On the subject of other benefits, the researchers suggest:

> Residents of supported housing are more likely to secure voluntary or paid employment . . . and to experience an improved quality of life. Investments in supported housing have also been shown to be associated with improved neighborhood quality and property values. Last, the social value of reduced homelessness, and of providing greater social protection for the disabled, while not possible to translate into economic terms, constitutes an important if less tangible benefit to society.
>
> Taken together, these unmeasured costs of homelessness and benefits of the housing intervention would have increased its already significant net benefit (and potential cost savings) were all such costs and benefits included in this study.[18]

The findings of follow-up studies supported these conclusions. Individuals in supportive housing used Veterans Administration services and were incarcerated less frequently than the homeless.

The Corporation for Supportive Housing has compared the relative costs of supportive housing and various forms of institutionalization. The cost of a psychiatric bed in state hospitals in New York City, Chicago, and San Francisco ranges from $290 to $383 per night, whereas the cost of supportive housing in these locations averages approximately $30 per night. A night in a San Francisco hospital psychiatric ward costs $570. A night in the city jail in any of these cities is two to three times that of supportive housing.[19]

These studies confirm what most would say is obvious: permanent housing for the homeless is cost-effective. So why are we less willing to pay for housing for the homeless when so many of us want the homeless off the street and when housing the homeless at public expense can actually save money? It is due in part to our moral ambivalence about public housing and particularly about publicly funded housing for the homeless. Public housing has a bad image. In the mid-twentieth century, the federal government built thousands of low-income units, but its cost-control mechanisms guaranteed that the housing constructed under its auspices would provide little more than shelter. The resulting large blocks of anonymous housing became decrepit and dangerous, engendering a widespread and persistent conviction that this was not a worthwhile expenditure.

Many feel that the homeless are not worthy of financial support, an attitude that dates back to the early days of shelters. The homeless are seen not as victims of circumstances, or as people with health problems, but rather as a class of individuals responsible for their own plight. In some cities there is such a dire need for affordable housing that even getting on the waiting lists obligates individuals and families to go through the homeless system. New York City has a bureaucracy that investigates those claiming to be homeless in order to ensure that they qualify for housing assistance. This perpetuates a view of the homeless as ne'er-do-wells trying to benefit from whatever society is doling out.

We need a shift in perception and strategy. This shift will be difficult, and it will take time—time to develop the programs, time to get people into them, time to let the programs work, and time to build the appropriate housing. It will also be difficult to redirect the effort and political will to apply public funds to this housing. We still need the police, emergency services, and jails, each of which spends resources on the homeless. It is unlikely that their budgets will be redirected toward building for the homeless: convincing any agency that its appropriations should be reduced because new homeless housing will decrease its workload is a hard sell.[20]

In order to shift strategies, we must first accept that the vast majority of homeless do not want to be homeless; many of the homeless do not have the capacity to extricate themselves from homelessness without assistance. Even if some are scamming the system, it is a small percentage—hardly enough to indict all the others and deny them assistance. Second, we need to acknowledge that we already spend public money on housing when we view the occupants as deserving, as is the case for students in public universities, or because doing so protects our quality of life, as in the case for prisoners.[21] Third, we need to change our approach away from spending large amounts of money in order to cover up homelessness and its effects—trying to make it invisible—and instead redirect our efforts toward solutions that will deal with the causes. This means building housing and support facilities.

THE ARCHITECTURAL PROGRAM 4

IN 1995 I BEGAN working on the design of an assisted care and after care facility for the Larkin Street Youth Center in San Francisco. I knew little about the intended residents except that they were all between 18 and 24 years old, were homeless, and were HIV-positive or had AIDS. The center's staff had been working with this group for some time and had very specific expectations about what kind of housing was needed, but this was the first such facility in the country, and there were no specific precedents to guide the building's design. What we needed was a program that would incorporate what we knew from prior experience, what would be required for the health and safety of the residents, and what was possible in the context of the building that we were renovating. This program also sought to satisfy the staff's expectations—although some of these were articulated only after we began design.

How is an architectural program different from design? The program is a document that guides the design decisions. Think of it as the outline for an essay: you know the topic, but you must define your thesis, your approach, your audience, the length, and the research you will need to support your points. In fact, designing is much like writing: you begin by articulating the requirements (program), you write an initial draft (the schematic), you refine that draft (design development), and you send it off for printing and publication (construction). I also like to think of the process of developing an architectural program as analogous to an eye exam. In the same way that the doctor tests different lenses by asking which view is clearer, an architect tests out ideas, approaches, and qualities among those who will use the space. The needs that the building is intended to satisfy come into clearer focus with every response.

Design decisions are based on a sharply defined set of criteria. The criteria for an architectural program may be prescriptive or based on performance. For example, a program might specify that the building must incorporate a classroom that measures 20 feet by 30; this is the *prescriptive* standard, which leaves little for the architect to interpret. A *performance* standard would declare that the space is intended for teaching, and that it must accommodate thirty people in various teaching formats (lectures, seminars, and small groups). The performance standard might also provide a list of expected qualities and features, such as natural light and ventilation, the room's capacity to be darkened for movies, and the availability of pin-up space on walls.

The architectural program incorporates not only requirements that define the physical space itself but also the various users' expectations about how the space will be used. Often these conflict, and it is the role of the architect (working with the client) to resolve the conflicts, set priorities, and establish the overall goals for the architecture.

The first question is always: Who is the client? Housing invariably must satisfy multiple clients. When building affordable housing and housing for the homeless, the sponsor, if not a city, is most likely a nonprofit developer or service provider whose main priority is the best interests of the ultimate occupants. But what the developer sees as being in the best interest of the occupant may not coincide with what that occupant views as important. The individuals served by the housing have little political power and little say in the design process (and more often none). At the early stages of the process, moreover, the actual future occupants are unknown; and even if they were known, their desires might not be representative of all those who will inhabit the housing over the building's lifetime. An architect may have access to a few prospective residents who can provide some insights, but their inputs tend often to be based on negative experience, defined as what they do *not* want, rather than what they do. Program information for some occupant groups is well documented in the literature, but for specific groups, such as young homeless people with AIDS, there are few available data on which to base a program.

The facility's neighbors constitute another group of clients. Very often they oppose the project altogether, fearing that the homeless pose a risk to public safety and the quality of life in the neighborhood, and they may exercise considerable political pressure to prevent its use as a shelter. Even those who tolerate the presence of housing for the homeless in their community want to minimize its size and impact. All those who work in the facility also have needs and wishes; they too are a client. Finally the clients include the sources of funding for the facility's construction, usually government agencies, each with their own requirements and expectations.

Shelters and transitional housing serve many types of homeless people, whose interests sometimes conflict, so different programs are required for particular forms of housing. Housing for youth with AIDS, abused women, seniors, or the mentally ill each entail distinct programmatic and spatial requirements. One significant source of conflict among the stakeholders is the residents' desire for privacy and the staffs' need to supervise the residents. Another is the desire to create a pleasant environment with a residential ambience while recognizing that these facilities cannot constitute a permanent home.

"FIRST PRINCIPLES" AND "PROFOUND INSIGHTS"

Since an architectural program is a time-consuming endeavor, entailing the synthesis of complex and even conflicting information, architects often rely on previously formulated programs for comparable projects. These are informally codified into general guidelines that are based on fieldwork and on similar circumstances. The problem with guidelines, however, is that they can address only one issue at a time, whereas design is multivariate. A simple guideline for designing shelters, for example, might posit that residents require privacy while they sleep; another might posit that shelter staff need to be able to monitor the sleeping area at all times. It is up to the architect to reconcile these conflicting requirements and set priorities.

Another way to develop a program is through the use of "first principles" and "profound insights." A first principle is a program element so well established through precedent and research that it constitutes the heuristics of a building type. In her classic 1961 book, *The Death and Life of Great American Cities,* Jane Jacobs recommended that urban housing incorporate windows that give a view onto the street so that residents can discreetly and continuously monitor activities within their neighborhoods. This became known as "eyes on the street" and over time evolved into a first principle of housing design.

A "profound insight" is based less on research and more on an architect's ability to understand, and be attuned to, the client's needs, even when these needs are not formally articulated. For example, Robert Herman, a San Francisco housing architect who has designed many projects for seniors, believes that their housing must make annual cycles evident. Changes in light, color, and climate are important because they represent the passage of time and its relationship to places—sensibilities that Herman believes are more developed among seniors than among younger people. Herman's designs (such as Mendelsohn house in San Francisco) often incorporate courtyards with fountains, annual flowering plants, and deciduous trees.

This chapter describes the most important program elements for various types of housing for the homeless, as well as some of the first principles and profound insights that inform the most successful of these projects.

EMERGENCY AND TRANSITIONAL SHELTERS

There is an old saying: "You only have one chance to make a first impression." Facilities that are impersonal, institutional, and threatening do little more than intensify the anxieties of homeless people who may be entering them for the first time; confronted with such a prospect, they are likely simply to turn around and leave.

THE ENTRY

When individuals become homeless, they feel many different emotions: anger, confusion, embarrassment, fear, exhaustion, depression, and hopelessness. Many are hungry, ill, or using drugs. The facilities that we design to house them therefore need to convey qualities of sanctuary and refuge at the outset, and the entry is critical in establishing trust between the homeless and the shelter staff. No single formula can convey these qualities in building design. The designer must try to understand how individuals arriving in a shelter (especially for the first time) might feel, and create a place that communicates an impression that it was designed specifically for them. When I began working on facilities for the homeless, my first instinct was to define the entry, reception, and interview areas as private spaces, reasoning that individuals who feel vulnerable, ill, or disoriented would be put at ease by a private meeting with a sympathetic person. But shelter workers indicated the contrary: the homeless want an open and public space.

FIGURE 34 The reception desk for an emergency shelter is a prominent part of the lobby. The staff can monitor the lobby, whose open plan defines it as a welcoming place.

Many who arrive at a shelter are unsure or suspicious of how the facility operates, and they want a visual assurance that the shelter is not a prison. They want to be able to look around, to see other people, and to understand what lies beyond the lobby. They study the bulletin board's announcements of activities, classes, and legal aid and health-care services. Meeting privately with a stranger would probably be more intimidating than comforting.

The reception desk itself has symbolic importance. Again my initial thinking was that a large desk would be impersonal and institutional, but the opposite is often true. A large counter staffed by more than one person (figure 34) suggests that the facility is well managed, and signals that it is safe and secure. Much, of course, has to do with the qualities of the facility's staff, which no amount of excellent design can replace, but a design that makes users feel invited, connected, and accepted defines a positive first step.

Facilities that serve such a varied population need to anticipate the unexpected and the unusual. The open, friendly entry must be paired with a place in which to retreat. Clients may be ill (emotionally or physically) when they arrive; others may be abusive or even dangerous; the staff needs a room in which to sequester these individuals until the situation stabilizes. If few staff are available, they will need some means, such as a window into the reception area, through which they can observe the lobby. In some instances the resident may not be the cause of the disruption; in youth facilities, for example, an irate or abusive parent may come looking for a runaway child. An open reception area is more than simply accommodation for the resident; it provides staff with a means of supervising activity, either visually or aurally.

The entry sequence, which includes intake and reception, serves another function as well: it is the facility's buffer from the community. One of the recurrent concerns expressed by neighbors opposing proposed homeless shelters is that the facility will encourage vagrancy and that those who await entry will loiter on the sidewalks. Program features that might mitigate these concerns include a courtyard (often gated), a large reception area, and a day room. The waiting begins in the courtyard, then moves indoors, minimizing the visual impact on the community.

Security is an important component, but so too is providing information. From a single station a staff member can both monitor the courtyard and the day room and field questions regarding the facility's hours of operation, services, and programs. Some facilities also have a coatroom, much like those one might see at a museum. Visitors can check a small bag or duffel for the day and retrieve it before the late-afternoon closing, thus avoiding the need to lug around belongings.

These program elements are not universal, however, and they pertain mostly to emergency and transitional shelters for single people of all ages without children. A shelter for families requires an area to accommodate children while the parent, usually the mother, is handling administrative issues. This area must be well supervised, and given the anxieties inherent in the situation (which would only be made worse by physical separation), parent and child need visual access to one another. In shelters that accommodate both women with children and single men, this sequence of entry and reception is invariably separate. Homeless women are fearful of men—often for good reason, since many have been raped or beaten while on the streets. Children are most often accompanied by their mother; two-parent families are rare among the homeless.

PUBLIC AREAS

One of the worst aspects of emergency shelters is waiting— for admission, food, a bed, or a shower. Most shelters have a day room, which serves as an alternative to sitting in a lobby or standing in line. In some instances, these are situated in drop-in centers that are physically separate from the shelter. In New York City, for example, all families seeking shelter must first go to the Emergency Assistance Unit in the Bronx, where they wait for an opening elsewhere. These day rooms serve two purposes. First, they are a refuge from the streets, providing a place in which social workers can make contact with their clients. Second, day rooms encourage socialization, in the same way as common rooms in senior centers or children's day-care facilities. People who come in from the streets are unlikely to have a social network or a sense of community. Living in permanent housing, obtaining and retaining employment, and simply negotiating daily life require social skills; access to a place in which they can meet others, forge friendships, find assistance, and feel safe is a beginning. The rooms also serve those who are not homeless. Neighborhood seniors come to play cards and be with friends outside the confines of their small apartments. Often there are two such rooms: a quiet room, and another in which conversation is encouraged. A television might seem an obvious feature, but as often as not there is none, since passive viewing tends to work against the beneficial social aspects of such spaces.

Little effort is expended in making such environments anything but institutional. Because the population is often rough, dirty, or drunk, the furniture is designed to withstand hard use; the room is often lined with lockers, distributed by lottery (since there are rarely enough lockers to fill the need), making the place seem like a bus terminal. Natural light humanizes space. The light can emanate from windows, skylights, or both. It can be direct, bringing in sunlight, or indirect, producing a soft, even light. Using natural light in day rooms is a relatively economical means of lighting the interior, and it has several benefits. First and foremost, natural light provides variety, changing during the course of the day and with the passage of the seasons; it reflects off walls, ceilings, and furniture. Homeless people spend much of their time seeking protection from the elements, but natural light connects them to the outside at the same time that the physical structure protects them from the harshness of the environment. The message, conveyed subliminally, is important: that the world outside can be tamed, and that individuals can control it by making choices about which elements to exclude or to admit.

Visual access between the outside and an enclosed communal space symbolically defines social connections. Homeless people still on the street can see their peers in a protected and safe sanctuary. For those within, the view to the outside suggests a choice, which is the cornerstone of dignity. Uniformity is the antithesis of choice; architecture provides a means to define choices visually, even within a single space. Variations in ceiling heights, for example, facilitate intimate groupings in a large space; low walls can define particular settings for different types of activities while making it possible to supervise the space in its entirety; different wall colors, floor finishes, and furniture create visual diversity within the room and encourage a corresponding variety of activities within.

In designing a daytime drop-in center for homeless youth in what had formerly been a furniture store, I inserted a large curving red wall highlighted with glowing yellow tubes as a means of defining several areas within a long narrow space (figure 35). At the entry, a low wall forms the reception counter. It then rises to full height, enclosing an office with windows. Finally it reverts into a partial wall, this time beginning at the ceiling and stopping seven feet above the floor to create a visual division between the recreation and dining areas. Case-worker offices, enclosed behind a bright yellow wall, have windows on both spaces; tucked beneath an existing stair is an intimate seating alcove with a view to the pool table (figure 36).

If storage is needed, lockers can be situated in an alcove, visible by the staff but separated from the main space. The lockers do not have to be drab and utilitarian; they too can be colorful. Other alcoves might include a telephone, or a bulletin board with information posted about jobs, activities, social services, legal rights, and housing opportunities. Access to a telephone and a mailing address are important elements of an employment search; for that reason, day rooms often incorporate a mailroom. In new shelters such as the Los Angeles Mission and the Union Rescue Mission, discussed in chapter 2, showers are available adjacent to the day room.

Often the public spaces are situated within the facility, rather than at its periphery, forming a transition from the public area to the more private inte-

FIGURE 35 The brightly colored curving wall in a drop-in center for homeless youth in San Francisco defines discrete spaces along its length.

rior and defining the center around which private activities revolve. The public space thus constitutes both a buffer and connection; it allows residents to retreat to their private domain, but it also draws them into their newfound community. In larger facilities that accommodate different populations (such as families with children, seniors, or the ill), each group may have its own public space, atrium, or even exterior courtyard. This space sometimes has a specific function (such as day care for children), but it is more often multipurpose, used for classes, special events, group meals, and meetings.

As in conventional housing developments, courtyards can be useful elements in facilities for the homeless, supporting particular functions and fostering a sense of community. Architecturally, courtyards bring light into the building's interior or provide sight lines into a controlled space. This is particularly useful when the context of the facility (a warehouse complex, a parking lot, or a busy street) constitutes an unpleasant visual prospect. Courtyards can also be a useful means of satisfying neighbors' objections to having facilities for the homeless in their midst, since they concentrate activity at the complex's interior and thereby reduce the facility's auditory and visual impact. In addition to serving as centers for communal activities and as buffers from "the street," courtyards can connect elements of the facility to one another; although particularly suited to temperate climates, they can be universally adapted to meet these various functions. In serving as a connection into the facility's private spaces, courtyards minimize the need for hallways, which are difficult spaces, both

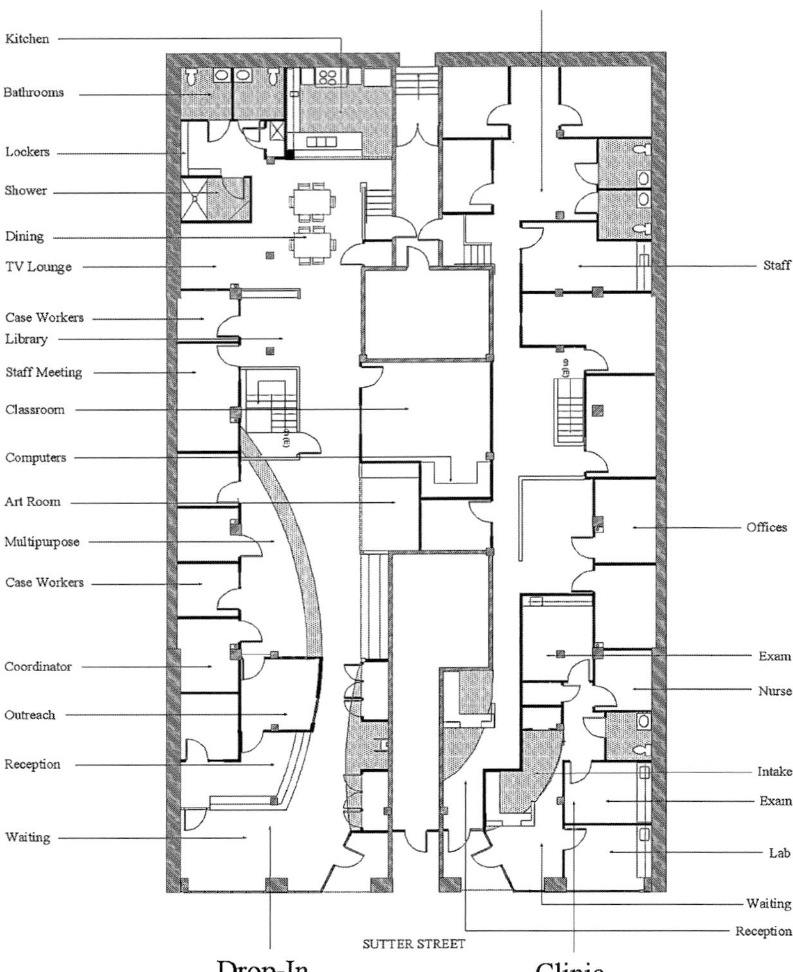

FIGURE 36 The reception area includes an enclosed office and two activity spaces at the back of this long and narrow formerly commercial space.

visually and functionally, since their sole function is to move people from one place to another. Perhaps most important, courtyards can make large facilities seem small.

HALLWAYS

Sometimes hallways are unavoidable. The size of the site might be small compared to the program, allowing little space for courtyards or atria; or the facility might be situated within an existing building whose geometry demands a more conventional corridor plan. In these cases, techniques employed to enliven corridors in other buildings work well. A single-loaded corridor, with rooms on one side and windows on the other, provides natural light, ventilation, and views to the outside as one moves through the building. If there are

FIGURE 37 This lounge opens to the hallway, from which passersby can see the activities within. Windows within the lounge bring natural light into the corridor.

public rooms among the more private spaces—a laundry room, lounge, or library—these can be open to the corridor, providing a view into the room, as well as to the outside from within (figure 37). This arrangement not only reinforces a sense of community by allowing passersby to participate in the activities taking place within the public rooms, but it also provides the corridor with visual diversity and interest.

Designing passageways that have views and easy access to other spaces is particularly important in homeless facilities. Facilitating freedom of movement and creating choices among several destinations are a recognition of the dignity of those who occupy the facility. Those who are not homeless have the option of moving from one room in their dwelling to another, or going outdoors, or being welcomed in a café. The homeless, in spite of the fact they are living outdoors, are largely deprived of such freedom of movement; by occupying a doorway or a niche between dumpsters (as the homeless often do), they are in fact seeking to carve out a private realm where they can stay.

As in all housing design, one of the architectural objectives in designing facilities for the homeless is to create a transition from public to private domains. Providing for degrees of privacy—a means of retreating into a private space—increases the sense of security associated with the dwelling.

SPECIALIZED SPACES

Some features and spaces are specific to particular populations; others are common to all. Most new facilities for the homeless, including transitional housing, contain areas intended for social services. The number and size of other components depend on the size of the overall facility and the character of the populations that it is intended to serve. The extent to which the following should be included will depend on the level of funding available, the size of the building to be constructed or renovated, the population served, and the nature of the services that will meet their needs.

Health Clinic

Nearly 80 percent of the homeless suffer from some type of health problem—either physical or emotional.[1] While it may not be economically feasible to staff a full-time, hospital-style clinic within a facility for the homeless, many shelters provide access to health-care specialists who regularly visit the facilities. The type of care often reflects the character of the facility's population: if the facility is for young women with children, a gynecologist and a pediatrician will make regular visits; homeless seniors often have access to gerontologists. The homeless may qualify for Medicare, but most have no other form of insurance, nor a regular primary-care physician. The clinic may be no more than a small waiting room, an examination room, a room for records, and another for triage. Some of the newer and well-funded shelters discussed in chapter 2 include full medical facilities resembling primary-care hospitals.

Access to health care is often made available to those not staying at the shelter as well. A separate entry allows the health-care facility to operate on a schedule different from that of the shelter's general activities. This separation may encourage the shelter-averse to use these services.

Smoking Lounge

Demographically, the percentage of smokers among the homeless and formerly homeless is very high, perhaps reflecting broader issues of addictive behavior among these populations. Facilities for the homeless do little to discourage smoking other than prohibiting it in interior public spaces, since other substance abuse problems are deemed more acute and immediately harmful. Most homeless facilities provide a specific area for smoking, partly in recognition of the prevalence of smoking among the homeless, but also as an accommodation to neighbors' concerns that in the absence of an alternative, shelter residents will loiter on public sidewalks to smoke.

Depending on the specific population, smoking areas can be discrete and private; often a small exterior court or atrium is designated as the smoking area. In most cases these areas need to be monitored (and thus viewable) by staff, particularly when the shelter's population contains a high proportion of drug or alcohol abusers, who in the absence of supervision might use the area to ingest explicitly prohibited substances.

Kennel

Another program element that is often overlooked in the design of facilities for the homeless is a kennel. Homeless young women in particular tend more often to have pets than do other homeless individuals, and they often cite the absence of facilities for their pets as a reason for avoiding shelters. A strong emotional attachment to a pet and the willingness to take responsibility for it are sentiments worth encouraging among the homeless, and kennels provide a means of accommodating these individuals while protecting the animals and other residents. In most cases, kennels are small, but they require good ventilation, floor drains, and water, and they are relatively costly to construct and to maintain.

Bank

The homeless are unlikely to have access to financial services. Most do not have bank accounts, and if they have a credit rating, it is unlikely to be sufficient to satisfy housing or purchasing needs. If the goal is to move the homeless to permanent housing, they will need the first month's rent and very often a month's rent in advance as a security deposit, which will have to be saved while at the shelter.

The lack of a checking or savings account creates several immediate problems for the homeless. Those who have jobs, as many homeless people in fact do, lack a secure place in which to deposit their earnings; those who receive public assistance are forced to use check-cashing outlets, which take a large percentage in exchange for the service they provide. In both instances, carrying money makes these individuals vulnerable to theft; individuals in recovery programs may be tempted to use the cash for drugs or alcohol.

Shelters often open an account on behalf of a resident at a local bank, but the presence of a banking facility within the shelter (often no more than a secure room with staff access) can form part of the process of integrating the homeless into a life of independence. Learning how to manage money and acquiring and maintaining credit are essential skills for shelter residents. Having a bank within the shelter is less intimidating for those not used to dealing with financial institutions than a bank outside the premises.

Courtroom

For the homeless, a courthouse is probably the most intimating of all institutions. Some may have outstanding warrants for minor quality-of-life crimes such as vagrancy, or for more serious offenses related to drugs and domestic violence. Homeless women often have child custody matters that require judicial intervention. It is not unusual for a homeless woman who is addicted to drugs or alcohol to have been separated from her children, who are placed in foster care. Once residents successfully complete rehabilitation programs, their first goal is often to get their children back. When shelter programs work as intended, individuals are ready to get on with a productive life, which generally includes employment. Employment forms, however, require social security numbers, which will reveal any outstanding warrants; these obstacles are often sufficient to trigger a regression of behavior.

For all these reasons, many shelters include a courtroom, where judges, bailiffs, and lawyers attempt to dispose of issues expeditiously. Often a judge will set a condition that if the person remains in a program and shows progress over a period of time, the charges will be dismissed. For those on the judicial side, who often volunteer their time, this system is a humane and efficient means of dealing with legal issues that would otherwise overwhelm the courtrooms and the court system. For the residents, it sends a message that people are willing to help them turn their lives around. It is not unusual, once a matter has been so disposed, that there is spontaneous applause from all those present. Shelter courthouses are often used to resolve child custody matters.

The homeless courts do not operate all day, and therefore a room designed specifically for this use would not be efficient. In most cases the courtroom can be set up in a classroom or other multipurpose space. It is important, however, that the accoutrements of a court be present. This is partly because of the formality of the proceedings—there must be a place for the judge, lawyers, court reporter, and bailiff—but also because the proceedings must be understood as being official, a perception that would be obvious were it in a courthouse but necessarily less so in this context.

Classrooms

If a new resident is capable and receptive, planning the future begins immediately upon arriving at a shelter. While much is imparted by the case manager in private, there are other components, such as group therapy for substance abuse, that require a sizable room. If the shelter is for youth, gaining a high school equivalency diploma is a first step. The character of classes will depend on the need, but the larger goal is to gain the skills that will enable a person to be employable and independent.

Because programs and approaches vary, a classroom needs to be flexible. Often sessions are held around tables, rather than in a formal lecturer-and-audience setting. Given the need to change configurations, an adjacent room for storing tables and chairs is particularly useful. There is often a separate computer lab, but computers can also be housed in commercially available cabinets that can be closed and pushed against a wall.

Beauty Parlor or Barbershop

Reestablishing self-esteem is an important component of overcoming homelessness. Individuals struggling to find shelter and food necessarily find it difficult to maintain personal hygiene and appearance. Often, however, the desire to look good is so strong, particularly among homeless women, that some are willing to spend much of their public assistance money at the beauty parlor. In recognition of this need, some shelter facilities include a salon, often staffed by volunteers.

The salon has another therapeutic value. Homeless women devote considerable effort to avoiding others while on the street. This leads to a sense of isolation and distrust, which works against receptivity to assistance; for that reason, many shelters and homeless service centers send a homeless person directly to the salon before any other intervention. The physical contact of having hair washed and cut does much to comfort fears and may establish receptivity to other types of assistance.

Gym

An exercise space has a similar objective, although this one appeals more to men. Homeless men, particularly those with substance abuse problems, are likely to have let their bodies deteriorate. Lack of good nutrition and regular sleep, combined with exposure to the elements, stresses the body. As other aspects of these individuals' lives improve, so too does their willingness to pay attention to their physical health. Regular exercise (particularly programmed exercise) is one component of establishing discipline and structure. Exercise that involves groups, such as basketball, also improves the ability to interact with others after years of isolation.

The larger the facility, the more elaborate and more sophisticated the exercise spaces. In many cases, the weight machines are donated by local gyms, replacing obsolete equipment.

Dining Room

The social component of a meal is as important as its nutritional purpose. In smaller shelters, particularly those for young people and mothers with children, sharing regular communal meals is a way of connecting with others in a relaxed setting, where procuring food is not the crisis that it is on the street.

Kitchens and communal eating spaces are generally physically adjacent and visually unobstructed from one another in order to define the preparation of food and the meal itself as shared activities. In several youth centers that I have designed, the service providers requested that the kitchen be accessible at all hours, so that residents would have the freedom to pour themselves a glass of milk or juice and have cookies whenever they liked. This simple feature (though in fact tempered by staff supervision of the kitchen) has enormous symbolic value: it declares that getting food when you want it is normal, and that this is a safe place like home, where such a freedom is a right.

In transitional shelters, food preparation and meals, like other programs and activities, are intended to foster independence through the acquisition of life skills. These are in fact very complex skills, however, which often make severe demands on the residents. Some shelters include a kitchen shared by several residents who may have their own rooms. These shelters resemble student housing, with suites of three or four individual rooms that share a common living area and kitchen. Sharing a kitchen takes real coordination and cooperation, even among those who are friends and highly socialized. For those have been homeless for some time, have no cooking skills, have specific eating habits and preferences, and have no intrinsic connections to the individuals with whom they are sharing the space, this arrangement is often unworkable.

In a New York City shelter for homeless people with HIV/AIDS built on this model, some residents began cooking by putting a pot on the stove, but then returned to their room to lie down, often feeling the effects of medication; they would fall asleep, leaving the pot to burn. Arguments often arise about the ownership of utensils and groceries, or the tidiness of the kitchen. For large shelters serving thousands of meals each day, this communal approach is not possible. In these cases the meals are less ritual and more necessity, and the venue is much more like those one would find in large college dormitories.

SLEEPING ARRANGEMENTS

The scope of activities sponsored by homeless shelters has expanded considerably over the last several decades, but one of the principal functions of shelters remains providing the homeless with a place to sleep. A night on the street, where the homeless are exposed to the elements and vulnerable to those who prey upon the weak, is a harrowing experience, but these feelings are not entirely put to rest by a night in a shelter. Shelters have long been perceived by the homeless as fraught with risks (as indeed these facilities were during the last hundred years): the risk that they will be violated, that they will fall prey to illness, that their belongings will be stolen, that they will feel imprisoned. Such fears are most acute at night, and sleeping spaces, for that reason alone, require particularly thoughtful design.

As has been the case for more than a century, dormitories remain the most common form of sleeping spaces in emergency shelters. The size of these facilities, many of which sleep more than a hundred, however, tends to militate against their intended function. Present-day health and safety codes, by mandating adequate ventilation and fire prevention measures, have done much to improve the quality of these facilities relative to their squalid precedents. But a dorm is a dorm, and for many, the experience of spending a night in an emergency shelter, in the company of sick, abusive, unhappy, or simply antisocial strangers, is probably little different from the prospect of a night in the notorious flophouses of the early twentieth century.

Contractors working on a renovation I designed in San Francisco that transformed an emergency shelter into a transitional facility were horrified at the hygienic conditions they found. Excrement was smeared on the walls, toenails (and worse) were found wedged between the bed frames and privacy screens. And all this in well-managed shelter that had been cleaned daily.

The young and the old, the chronically ill and the healthy, the sober and the intoxicated often share a single dormitory in emergency shelters; segregation is most often limited to providing separate accommodation for men and women, although in some shelters even this has proved problematic. While working on my first adult shelter in the 1990s, I toured several other facilities and kept hearing references to the "24 and 7 rule"; I had no clue what this meant. Heterosexual couples seeking overnight accommodation in a shelter must sleep separately; the segregation rule becomes complicated, however, with respect to transsexual clients, who are not rare in San Francisco Bay Area shelters. Men who have been separated from their female companions are suspicious of a transsexual individual sharing space in the women's dormitory, and they are no less sanguine at the prospect of sharing sleeping accommodation with an individual whom they perceive as homosexual. One solution demands that transsexuals declare their gender and live it twenty-four hours a day, seven days a week: "24 and 7." Another solution that avoids the problem is a separate dormitory for transsexual clients. This supplemental dormitory is flexible by design; in the absence of transsexual clients on a given night, it can be used to house men or women, depending on the demand, or it can be used to house people with particular needs, such as the mentally ill, individuals with communicable diseases, the intoxicated, or drug users when safety considerations make it necessary to segregate them.

Emergency and transitional shelters are increasingly dividing large dormitories into separate sleeping spaces. The benefits are several. Smaller sleeping quarters enable residents to exercise some degree of control over their environment. The ability to divide up the sleeping space also benefits management, particularly in emergency shelters, where the specific character of the population may change from one night to the next. By creating flexible groupings of ten to twenty beds, staff can assign space in the most appropriate manner where it is needed.

Fixed physical divisions of the dormitory space, with each group assigned a discrete room, necessitate a larger supervisory staff, which is rarely possible given the limited resources of most emergency shelters. The sleeping quarters in transitional shelters, which typically accommodate the homeless for longer periods than do emergency shelters (and thus have a more stable population), lend themselves to more permanent physical divisions.

When it is not possible or advisable to create permanent separate sleeping rooms, several means, including temporary walls, permanent low walls, and cabinetry, are available to create discrete and private areas in large dormitories. The particular design solution is a function of cost, the extent of the change desired, and the need for storage. In the early 1990s Asian Neighborhood Design, a San Francisco nonprofit architecture and development organization, converted a San Francisco warehouse into a homeless shelter. For the dormitory area, the group designed and constructed (in its cabinet shop) an integrated, simple, and flexible system of demountable partitions and bed frames (figure 38) that had three anticipated advantages:

FIGURE 38 Low partitions in this San Francisco shelter provide a modicum of privacy and support the bed frame. They can also be reconfigured, although they are rarely moved.

(1) the devices could be manufactured while the space was being renovated and then easily assembled on-site; (2) the arrangement of the beds could be altered by the staff as necessary; and (3) the system could be used in many different locations. The bed frame stabilizes the partitions, keeping them in position, while the partitions serve the dual purpose of providing vertical support for the beds and ensuring the privacy of each occupant. Under each bed is a lockable box drawer for personal storage. The entire device is made of wood, and the partitions have a laminate veneer that is easily cleaned. The flexibility afforded by off-site manufacture and the adaptability of the system to different facilities have proved the most successful elements of the Asian Neighborhood Design system; once in place, however, the bed partitions are not often moved (against expectation), since they are heavy, unwieldy, and more difficult to assemble than anticipated. Elements of the bed partitions have proved vulnerable—in particular the strips of wood that cover the plywood edges, and the screw-on adjustable feet, which tend to shear off if the assemblages are dragged across the floor. Nevertheless, the system has worked well. It has withstood years of hard wear and is still in use in some facilities.

The need for flexibility is greater on a daily cycle in emergency shelters because of the uncertain demographics of the population on any given night; at the same time, it is simply not feasible to reconfigure the space every day. In such instances, permanent divisions within sleeping areas are a better solution. The number of beds within a specific area is based on several criteria and constraints, including the size of the overall space, the extent to which it can be efficiently divided, the number and variety of spaces needed, and the extent to which the entire space can be monitored by one or two staff members. There is no magic

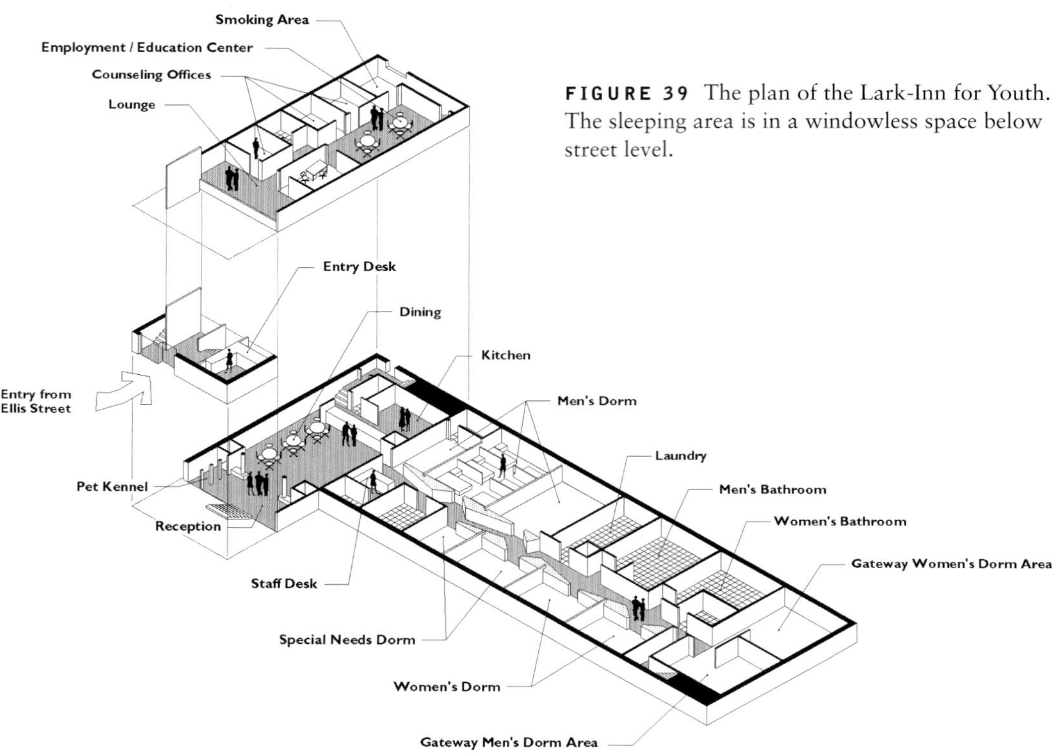

FIGURE 39 The plan of the Lark-Inn for Youth. The sleeping area is in a windowless space below street level.

number, but experience indicates that dividing large spaces into units accommodating groups of eight to ten people allows for a relatively high degree of privacy while facilitating the development of a sense of community among the residents. Determining the size of these groups is guided as much by the intent to facilitate cooperative decision-making as by the physical constraints of the space. This is particularly true in transitional facilities, where much of the psychology of transitioning consists of forming social connections and learning appropriate norms of social behavior.

In a forty-bed shelter that I designed for Larkin Street Youth Services, I divided a large windowless space into a set of eight smaller dormitories (figures 39 and 40). Because no one knew how many clients would arrive on a given day, the facility needed the flexibility that this number of different spaces provided. As it turned out, this was a prudent decision, not only because the number of residents varied, but also because, as several of the clients stayed in the shelter for longer periods (sometimes six months or even more), the need for supervision decreased. The two dormitories (one for men, the other for women) situated farthest from the staff desk are called the "gateway dorms"; each has access to a separate (rarely used) entry and its own bathroom, with a bathtub as well as a shower. The two dormitories have fewer beds than the others and are more comfortably furnished. Residents of the gateway dorms are nearing total independence and the ability to live in permanent housing; they have jobs, they are relatively self-reliant, and their progress through the

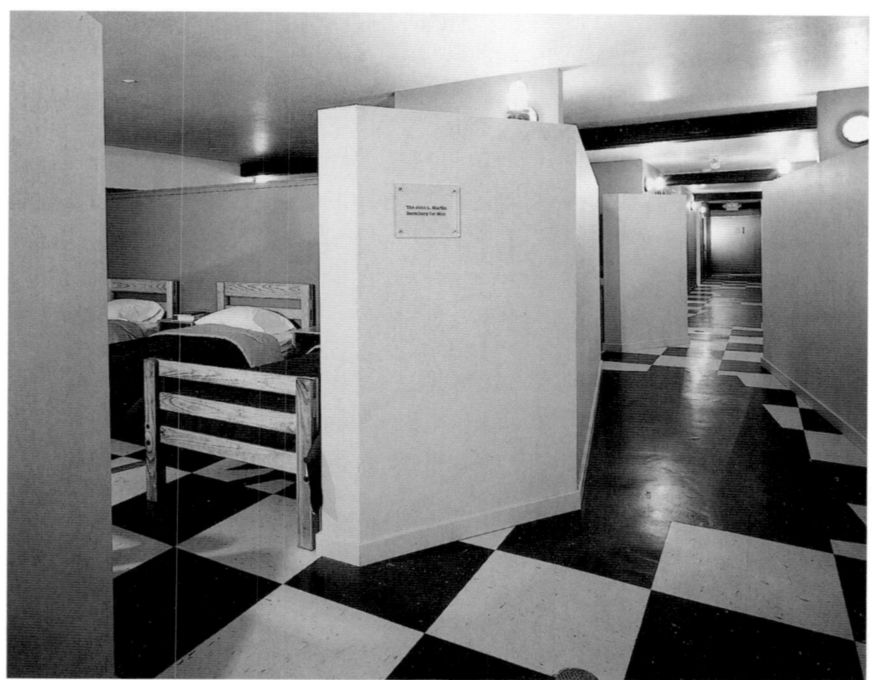

FIGURE 40 The dormitory of the Lark-Inn for Youth. Each smaller area has six to eight beds, permitting flexibility in the assignment of sleeping spaces. At the entry to each dormitory unit, accessed from an irregularly shaped hall, the floor pattern and color change.

program has entitled them to a higher degree of privacy than new clients. The gateway dorm is the last step in their transition to independence.

The main design difference between a transitional shelter and an emergency facility, even when each is accommodated within the same structure, is the number of people sleeping in the same space and how much storage each person has in immediate proximity to the bed. These distinctions correspond, in social terms, to the extent to which residents have control over their space and the number of people (more precisely, how few) with whom they are obligated to negotiate. The more private accommodations serve two functions: First, increasing the extent of the individual's control of his space introduces the notion that physical space is a commodity that has value, since space represents an individual's needs, desires, and preferences. A person who has been homeless for some time, or has been in an emergency situation, is not likely to make this association. Making personal transitions visually apparent is part of the process of defining the progress to independence. Second, negotiating and coordinating basic personal preferences with others are skills that continue to be necessary after life in the shelter; individuals who have transitioned out of temporary shelters are likely to find themselves sharing permanent housing with others, simply because their finances often preclude entirely independent accommodations. Operators of transitional shelters understand these economic realities and shape their programs and living arrangements accordingly.

The design of the dormitory space for the Larkin-Inn for Youth (a wordplay on Larkin Street Youth Services) was intended both to encourage camaraderie among its residents and to facilitate their progressive socialization. In the same way that the spaces at the extremes of the dormitory are an affirmation that their occupants are nearing independence, the space closest to the main entrance into the dormitory, where the staff desk is located, is reserved for those who require maximum supervision, either because of illness or behaviors.

The walls that divide these dormitories are six feet high, stopping several feet short of the ceiling. This is only partly to mitigate construction costs (full-height ceilings require more extensive ventilation and additional fire sprinklers); more important, the abbreviated walls are a means of providing privacy to the residents while ensuring that staff have the ability to supervise the space. The residents' privacy is not absolute in these accommodations (doors have been deliberately omitted from the design), but neither is the staff's ability to monitor the residents: direct sight lines into the spaces are limited. The low walls do not enable staff to see directly into each space, but rather give the impression that they can.

The dormitory at the Lark-Inn for Youth occupies a basement that was once a nightclub. The windowless space is large, long, and narrow. The walls that define the dormitory units are not straight in plan but project at angles into a hall that connects them. The intent was to provide some variety and to avoid a long continuous hallway, which would have drawn attention to the configuration of the space and made it seem institutional. The angles of these walls create enlarged areas outside the entry to each dorm—a threshold space like a small plaza along a street. The thresholds are reinforced by a change in the color of the floor tile, creating zones of transition along the corridor and minimizing the perceived length of the hall (see figure 40).

Light fixtures are mounted at the top and sides of the low walls that define the entry to each of the eight dormitory spaces, providing varying intensities of light along the corridors. The light is brighter at the small plazalike spaces, diminishing the impression of a single long space and marking out the eight dormitories as a sequence of neighborhoods along a "street." The walls that define these smaller dormitories have electrical outlets adjacent to each bed, allowing the occupants to have a reading light, a clock radio, or a CD player with headphones; the configuration of adapted spaces, however, sometimes makes individual electrical outlets impracticable.

Lighting in Dormitories

The intent of limiting the number of people in one sleeping area is to provide them with some control over their environment. The ability to control light is a corollary of this principle, but it creates practical difficulties, since these mini-dormitories are most often part of a larger space. The spaces require ample ambient light for cleaning, reading, and other activities that take place during nonsleeping hours; at night, they need to be sufficiently illuminated to enable people to navigate among them without intruding on the other residents' ability to get to sleep. Ideally each person should have a night-light for reading, but this is rarely possible, and shelter staff worry that it could lead to disputes between residents who want stay up reading and those who are sensitive to light when they are trying to sleep.

The solution usually entails two different lighting systems, one of which can be adjusted with dimmers to illuminate the space with a low-level and soothing light throughout the night and the other a daytime system of higher-output lighting. Another solution is to maintain a continuously low level of light (adjustable if necessary) throughout the dormitory and to illuminate the passageways more brightly. Ceiling lighting is efficient, but it is likely to seem institutional. Wall lighting and indirect lighting, particularly if they can be controlled by dimmers, are a good alternative.

Case-Manager Offices

Emergency and transitional housing for the various profiles of homeless populations are one part of the road to self-sufficiency. The support features and facilities vary, but they invariably include case management. Each person entering the system is assigned a counselor who guides the client through the ever-increasing homeless bureaucracy, directing him or her to the appropriate services.

Case-manager offices need to be visible and accessible. In emergency shelters, the case managers often have private offices on the dormitory floor, with views over the dormitory and lounge areas. This serves two functions: it provides general supervision of the space, while making it evident to clients that assistance is near. Individuals with substance abuse problems and the emotionally disturbed are not in a position to make an appointment when they need help: help needs to be available at all times. In instances where the shelter facility is a secondary or adapted use, the space's geography often makes such physical proximity impossible. The case managers are on a different floor, often near or off a lobby. This physical separation creates a different dynamic between the case manager and residents. The case manager becomes more like a consultant or an outside social worker. Residents need to make a concerted effort to visit their case manager, rather than seek help on impulse.

THE STUFF

The homeless, like all of us, acquire items for various reasons. They collect some things to sell and others to use, including drugs (illegal and prescription), cigarettes, alcohol, and food. Like all of us, they need blankets, shoes, and clothing. As these items accumulate, however, keeping them becomes a problem for the homeless. Items need to be stored or carried around, which usually entails a shopping cart; these are plentiful, easily available (although their appropriation may constitute theft), and therefore the container of choice. Groups of homeless people sometimes pool their resources to rent a storage space near a location where they access services. This storage space sometimes doubles as a sleeping space.

The importance of stuff is much the same for the homeless as it is for people with homes; it may in fact be *more* important since these items constitute all their possessions. Those who are not homeless may have strong attachments to particular items, but they also know that they can replace them in most cases; they know that their possessions are relatively safe or that they can be protected by insurance. The confiscation of homeless people's shopping carts and their contents—a commonplace occurrence—can be devastating.

Some of the stuff that homeless people carry around with them is essential to their ability to manage their lives: this of course includes money if they have it, but also papers and documents required to gain access to general assistance funds, Medicare, and other services. Stuff might also include memorabilia of their lives before homelessness, an important connection to a more stable life and an incentive to work for its return. Often, however, there is no clear rationale for all of the stuff. Workers in San Francisco's Department of Public Works find the contents of many confiscated carts harrowing: in addition to drugs and needles, the carts and their contents are sometimes smeared with excrement, and many are infested with vermin.

Some homeless people find a way to store carts in public areas, using bicycle locks to attach them to a tree or a parking meter and protecting their contents with tarps. During the daytime, carts line the sidewalks of a street bordering People's Park in Berkeley, a haven for the homeless. Some homeless people refuse to go to a shelter or other facility if their entry is conditioned on parting with their belongings. Dealing with the stuff, therefore, is a necessary part of designing for the homeless.

Among the categories of stuff is contraband, the storage of which poses particular difficulties. Many homeless people have drug and alcohol abuse problems; "wet shelters" do not require that their residents be drug or alcohol free, reasoning that if they did, fewer people would come and fewer would be helped. Wet shelters do require, however, that residents not use drugs or alcohol while in the facility. Drugs, and the paraphernalia used to prepare or consume them, must be locked away in a secure, separate room (furnished with individual lockers or secure storage bins) to which residents can gain access only in the presence of staff. In addition to ensuring that contraband is not used within the facility, this system provides some assurance that the items will not be stolen. Publicly accessible lockers or storage cabinets can be broken into.

Weapons constitute another form of contraband. Some homeless people feel that they need weapons to survive on the street. This is a difficult choice for homeless service providers. They do not condone the use of drugs or weapons, but they are not the police. If they were to require residents to forgo these items altogether, many homeless people would simply not come to the shelter. They also need to provide a safe and civilized environment for everyone, so often the compromise (and the first step in gaining their client's trust) is to suspend judgment, remove the items, and place them in secure storage.

There are three other categories of stuff to be stored: household items, clothes, and personal items used at night (such as eyeglasses and books). The need for storage is acute in transitional shelters whose residents intend to move into permanent housing and may have accumulated many possessions during their extended stay. Residents need only limited access to these household items, but their storage is made complicated by the nature and size of the items; the issue is a relatively new development, as transitional facilities increasingly become the standard form of shelter for the homeless. Smaller appliances such as an iron, cooking utensils, or a radio can be stored on shelves in a separate secure room. Larger items, such as televisions, are more troublesome to store; if the shelter has several hundred residents, the storage facilities may need to be quite large. It may be that off-site storage is the best solution, saving space in the facility that can be better used for programs.

When the prospect of employment (including job interviews) arises, residents need appropriate clothing, such as a well-ironed dress or a sports coat, and they need a closet in which to store these clothes. Personal items need to be available at night but stored away in the daytime. Individual cabinets and closets need to be situated within the sleeping area, accessible frequently and at will, but still securable. In addition to clothing, storage needs to accommodate the items that one would typically find on a nightstand—eyeglasses, medicines, a water glass, reading material, and a clock—as well as toiletries and bedtime items, such as bathrobes and slippers. During the daytime, all of these items need to be locked away. Sometimes a conventional nightstand is the best solution, particularly when the sleeping area is divided into smaller spaces with a greater degree of individual control and oversight. Sometimes the closet, nightstand, and bed are manufactured as a single unit that specifically envisions storage needs. Devices that combine several storage functions can also serve as privacy screens between residents.

In some cases all three solutions—permanent walls, demountable privacy screens, and wardrobes—may be used simultaneously. When redesigning a San Francisco emergency shelter dormitory into a transitional facility known as Next Step, I used the Asian Neighborhood Design movable screens partly because they supported the beds, which had to be retained because of budgetary constraints, but also because even after ten years, they were in workable condition. To these I added permanent walls that divide the hundred-person dormitory into spaces for sixteen or fewer. These spaces are further divided into groups of eight by six-foot-high cabinets.

Episcopal Community Services, the shelter operator, specified several requirements for these cabinets, the most important being that each include a closet in which a sports coat, pants, or dress could hang. The cabinets also needed to incorporate a headboard, a nightstand, and general storage, as well as to provide privacy for the residents. They had to be sturdy, lockable, and easy to clean. To the client's requirements, I added my own. First, the cabinets had to create a sense of individuality; we couldn't make each unique (that would have been too costly), but each had to be clearly associated with one person even when grouped together. Second, I felt that the cabinets needed to have a collective presence: these lively forms, rather than the individual beds, should be the dominant element within the space. The shelter's operator wanted to make the large space seem more intimate (it had once been a car dealership) and proposed the analogy of "villages" for the dormitory. The cabinets, designed as archetypal house forms that collectively resemble a cluster of small buildings, express this village analogy visually (figures 41 and 42). Each cabinet, when placed back-to-back with another, forms a gable, and its sloping roof has the dual advantage of preventing dust from collecting on the top and discouraging residents from storing items on the cabinets, which could be dangerous and unsightly.

The upper part of the cabinet is divided into shelves for folded items and a closet. The latter is unusual in that the clothes hang parallel to the cabinet door. The design of the closet was dictated by the fact that a conventional closet (with a pole that permits clothing to hang perpendicularly) must be at least twenty inches deep; the size of the space and its configuration, however, could not have accommodated the requisite number of beds and cabinets had the cabinets been deeper. To make each item of clothing visible, the bracket attached to the back of the cabinet slopes downward, following the path of the cabinet's sloping top, so that each item hangs slightly below the one behind (figure 43). The entire upper part of each cabinet has a bi-fold door that can be secured with a padlock. The bi-fold design allows the entire upper cabinet to be opened from the side of the bed, without obstructing the passageways. Since some beds are entered from the right and some from the left, these doors are reversible.

The space below the enclosed cabinet is left open, except for a panel in the middle that serves as a headboard so residents can read in bed, comfortably supported. On either side of this panel is an open shelf, high enough for a glass of water, a clock, or other items that one might need during the night. This part is not lockable, so items of value must be stored in the closet during the day. The area below this shelf is additional lockable storage, accessible from the passageway; most residents use this space to store a suitcase or duffel bag. Items can also be stored beneath the bed.

I worried that having three separate padlocks

FIGURE 41 The dormitory in the Next Step transitional shelter is separated into private areas by demountable partitions, low permanent partitions, and cabinets.

FIGURE 42 Each resident has a lockable cabinet. When linked together, these cabinets form shapes resembling a village of small houses.

FIGURE 43 The individual cabinets serve as closet, general storage, headboard, and nightstand.

might prove a financial burden for the residents and require them to memorize many numbers. I considered having all three locks openable by a single key, but the staff was adamant that this would not work. Managing keys is a hassle, but, more important, residents felt that key locks could be picked, or that staff might have keys and therefore access to personal items (paranoia runs high among residents). In the end the padlocks worked fine, although the bi-fold doors are the weak link. Any mechanism that requires some level of care in its operation is going to be a problem, and the bi-fold doors are set in a track that keeps them attached to the cabinet; they sometimes stick or jump off the track.

The cabinets were manufactured at a unit cost of $450, an expense that satisfied Episcopal Community Services since the cabinets served several functions. The client had originally envisaged a more conventional closet cabinet (the doors of which would be accessed from the passageway) at the foot of each bed. This design had several advantages, including optimal access to the closet's entire height for hanging clothing, while the cabinet's back (which faced the bed) could serve as a headboard, perhaps incorporating a shelf. The disadvantage of this design was that the cabinets did not connect back-to-back, which made them less sturdy than the design that was ultimately chosen.

These cabinets would also have required a finished surface on the side facing the bed, which would have added to the cost.

These devices seem to work well, and the associations of their houselike form are recognized and appreciated (by some at least). Many residents have begun to personalize their spaces and the cabinets; some women call the cabinets their "Barbie houses" and populate them with their collections of stuffed animals. Some residents attached hooks to the sides to hang a robe, a feature that I should have anticipated and included at the outset. The staff has barred the practice, however, feeling that the hanging clothes constricted the passageways and made the dormitory look untidy. I liked it and felt that it showed initiative toward making the system work for each person.

TRAINING FACILITIES

Transitional homeless facilities increasingly offer their clients employment training as part of their programs. This may require that teaching spaces or computer labs be incorporated in the facility's design, but the training often requires more complex spaces, such as a commercial kitchen. Restaurant training works on many levels. In job-training terms, restaurants constitute an important service sector in cities, and they offer jobs at various levels of skill. Kitchens also provide meals for the facility and often for other service providers, including those who bring food to the house-bound. Finally, food preparation entails many of the socially defined qualities—self-reliance, hygiene, and service to others—that transitional shelters seek to develop among their clients.

Large commercial teaching kitchens, however, are expensive. The building code requirements are exhaustive, covering nearly every aspect of the space, including the materials used for flooring and the type of paint applied to the walls, as well as more obvious health-and-safety standards, such as the position and capacity of exhaust hoods, the materials used for countertops, the placement and capacity of refrigerators, the number, size, and type of sinks, and the configuration of the facility's plumbing. Transitional facilities often supplement these provisions with their own requirements, which take into consideration the health and safety of their clients: sharp utensils, for example, need to be kept locked in a drawer, and clients' access to food storage units is usually restricted. Despite the expense, food service is an increasingly common employment training option in transitional facilities.

Construction and specialized crafts also figure prominently among employment training programs in transitional facilities. Asian Neighborhood Design developed a cabinetry and woodworking program in San Francisco that offers training to the homeless and provides finished products to contractors. Another obvious work-and-training program is building maintenance, linked in many instances to the shelter's physical plant and management.

Often out-of-work residents of a shelter are hired to perform shelter maintenance. The social dynamics of homeless housing programs sometimes give rise to a delicate balance between staff and residents. Although peer pressure, particularly in transitional shelters, to some extent encourages residents to adhere to regulations, the authors and enforcers of rules and norms of behavior are ultimately the facility's employees. When residents become employees (even for part of a day), the dynamics of their relationship with other residents change and sometimes even give rise to conflicts. Some programs, recognizing the benefits of enabling residents to learn building management skills, take on increasing responsibility, and earn money, send residents to other homeless facilities for this work.

Support facilities within transitional shelters (such as beauty parlors, courtrooms, or banks) have tasks related to their operation that are often undertaken by residents as a means of establishing a proprietary stake in the facility, as well as a means of acquiring job skills.

MATERIALS

The maintenance of facilities is a function of the choice of materials used in their construction. Most facilities, whether emergency, transitional, or permanent housing for the homeless, operate under very tight budgets. Funds could, in principle, be spent for more durable materials, but larger budgets are more often used to construct larger facilities—not sturdier ones.

The materials used in housing for the homeless are generally identical to those used in multifamily housing. On the interior, these include gypsumboard walls and ceilings, vinyl tile floors, and plastic-laminate countertops in bathrooms. To the extent that extra funding is available, it is usually spent on upgrading the floors, or substituting ceramic tiles for vinyl in kitchens and bathrooms. These are all legitimate materials, but they often do not tolerate heavy use (or abuse), which is to be expected in facilities for homeless. Gypsumboard walls in particular can be easily damaged; it takes little effort to kick a hole in these walls. Hard-use design is not limited to facilities for the homeless; facilities that I have designed for college fraternities raised similar use issues. But these facilities, because they are used so intensively, need constant maintenance. At the very least, a well-run shelter needs to be thoroughly cleaned every day.

When budgets allow, indestructible materials are preferred. New shelters built during the early 1990s in New York City were constructed to an "institutional" standard, comparable to school or prison construction, but they cost \$200 per square foot or more—about twice the cost of new apartments.[2] These facilities, with concrete-block walls and ceramic tile or concrete floors, are wearing reasonably well, but they clearly do not feel residential. Even in these buildings, the selection of some items was guided by price, not durability. Standards were lower for cabinets and counters, and these ended up being the first items that needed replacement.

The same principles apply to the design and selection of furniture. The items available to the general public through large retail stores that specialize in mass-produced, partially assembled furniture, although stylish and cost-effective, will not work in most shelter contexts; they simply are not sturdy enough to withstand hard use by many different residents. The plastic-laminate finishes often chip, and legs tend to snap off when the item is moved. Often the furniture is too large for the small spaces. Furniture made of solid wood or covered with floor linoleum rather than plastic laminate is available, and some has been created expressly for use in shelters. Aura Oslapas of San Francisco has designed a complete line of furniture that includes beds with storage below, dressers with a slim profile to save floor space and stainless steel adjustable legs. Upholstered items, such as sofas and lounge chairs, have to be similarly sturdy. Arms are the most vulnerable and therefore are often not upholstered. Solid-color cushions show dirt and stains more readily than do bright patterns.

SIZE MATTERS, OR SMALL IS BEAUTIFUL

Those who operate facilities for the homeless most often recommend limiting their size to no more than forty people, for reasons similar to those advanced for keeping school class size small. Smaller size allows for more supervision and personal attention. Life on the street breeds isolation and suspicion of others (a reasonable survival strategy under the circumstances), and the homeless often have difficulty interacting with larger groups as a result. Certain populations, particularly those with certain types of mental illness, need a supportive environment that is not oppresive (as large shelters often are). Smaller shelters are likely to be perceived as having less impact on the neighborhood than would large complexes.

As the size of a facility increases, so too does its institutional and impersonal character. Smaller shelters lend themselves more easily to an architectural style that feels residential and welcoming, but shelters that are too small can compromise the efficiency of providing services, since they tend to work against economies of scale. Larger shelters, by contrast, have efficiencies of space, staff, and financing that enable them to provide a broader range of educational, medical, exercise, and training services to their clients.

The most common strategy for making a large shelter seem small is to segment the space into smaller components, an approach that physically parallels the transitions associated with an individual's progress through the shelter's programs. A greater degree of privacy or increased access to amenities generally involves moving into another, often self-contained area of the facility. Many large shelters signal this transition as an ascent through the building, with the higher floors corresponding to greater degrees of independence. Others signal these transitions in separate structures, sometimes arranged around individual courtyards.

"How big is too big?" is a recurrent question in all forms of housing, but it is a particularly important question in the design of affordable housing. During the 1950s, it was common practice to construct a sequence of identical buildings, each containing hundreds of living units, on a single site; the facelessness and brutality of this approach have informed the largely negative view of "public housing." A more recent approach has concentrated on smaller projects that fit comfortably into neighborhoods, and this approach is a sound one for shelters.

IMAGE

Using institutional or inexpensive materials does not mean that the facility has to be drab and impersonal. Varied lighting (both natural and artificial), diverse spaces, freedom of movement, and color can make a shelter environment feel accommodating and residential. One recurrent design dilemma is the principle that an emergency or transitional shelter should be inviting and comfortable but that it cannot (and should not) be "home." If it were, there would be less incentive for the residents to move on, which is the intent of transitional housing

What should be the image of a shelter? Each facility is different, either because of its geographic location and its placement within a city, or because of the intended residents for whom it has been designed. Architects must be free to interpret the program requirements of their clients, but architects also need to recognize that shelters are a building type that will require ongoing thinking, not only because we are learning about what works, but also because shelters will be needed for many years to come. The next chapter describes several examples of how architects have responded to this question.

PERMANENT HOUSING

Emergency and transitional shelters share a common theme in that neither is intended as a permanent housing solution for its residents; both restrict the length of their residents' tenure, with the ultimate goal of moving their clients into permanent, stable housing.

Sometimes (although circumstances make it unfortunately rare) the goal is to place clients into the existing housing market. In high-cost cities such as San Francisco this is extremely difficult; even in the relatively affordable Chicago area, the fair-market rent for a two-bedroom unit was $891 per month in 2002, which requires an hourly wage equivalent to $17 per hour; the minimum wage during that year was only $5.15 per hour.[3] Even with subsidies, some landlords are reluctant to rent to individuals coming from the shelter system. In New York, the permanent housing options are often so grim that some prefer to stay in the shelter. By 2002, the city's growing shelter population compelled officials to seek legal means to force those who qualified for permanent housing to accept such housing when available.[4]

Increasingly, service providers and nonprofit developers are creating new housing aimed at those graduating from shelters. In some cases, known as "housing first," this new housing is for the chronically homeless coming directly from street homelessness. The concept is that by placing them into housing with support services there will be reduced pressure on the police, public health workers, and hospital emergency rooms. Often specifically designed for populations with particular needs and requirements, such as those with mental illnesses, this new housing takes several forms, including conventional apartments. A large number, however, are single-room occupancy hotels (SROs), in which modest private units are combined with on-site services.

PROTOTYPE SROS

When projects are constrained by their program and budgets (as most of them are), a common trend is to codify and standardize. Sometimes design time and fees can be reduced by replicating a building type. The most obvious example is the fast-food restaurant. Corporate headquarters develops a prototype, sometimes using an architect, which can be built throughout the country once appropriate sites are procured. Several prototypes may emanate from the same program in order to accommodate different types of locations, such as urban and suburban sites. Tract homes, which buyers select from a limited set of predesigned models, are often developed in this way.

In developing a prototype, the architect's role is to refine the program needs, codify these as a set of requirements, and prepare a range of possible responses, anticipating the likely circumstances. The architect may in fact have no role in designing the actual building; another architect will be hired locally, or if the prototype is sufficiently specfic, only a builder may be needed. The need to provide housing for the homeless has become so acute recently that there is pressure to create prototypes and apply them quickly. Service providers, many of whom have little front-end development money to pay architects to design a unique building, can use the prototype to begin the process, procure funding, and shorten the required time. Government agencies can pay a single design fee for several buildings based on a single program and prototype.

One of the most thorough examples of this approach is New York City's *Design Manual for Service-Enriched Single-Room Occupancy.* This document establishes a prototype SRO specifically designed for those with mental illnesses. The design of the prototype SRO incorporates two main parameters: budget restrictions defined by the state's Office of Mental Health (initially about $60,000 per bed) and the residents' favored unit type: small, fully equipped independent units.

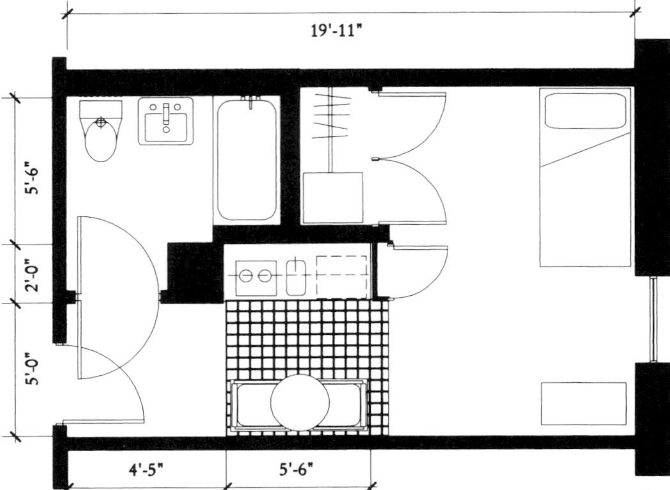

FIGURE 44 Plan of the supportive housing prototype studio. Each unit has an entry area, an eating area that also serves as circulation, kitchen and bath, and main room. Because there is no view of the bed from the entry, the unit feels larger and there is ample privacy for such a small space.

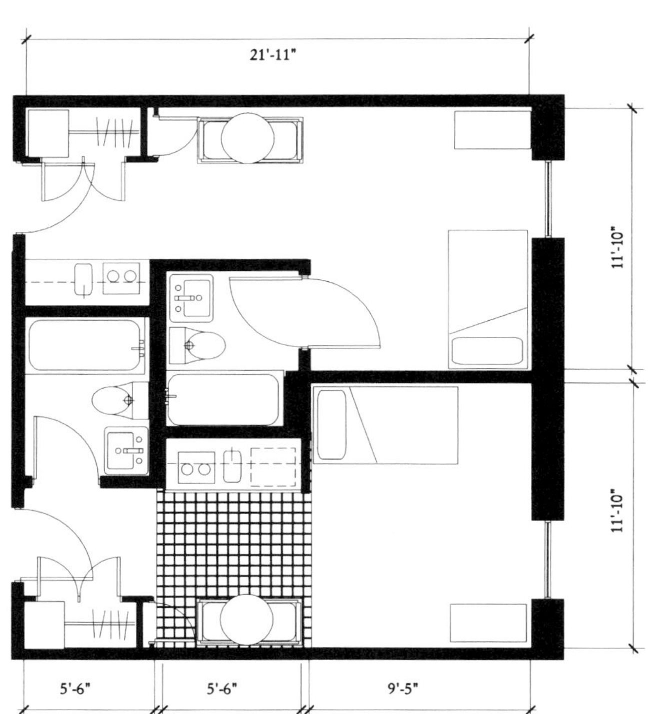

FIGURE 45 Prototype studios nestle together tightly around a core, which contains plumbing areas.

Richard Olsen, an environmental psychologist, established these user preferences by undertaking a postoccupancy evaluation of two existing facilities. Olsen interviewed former residents of two SRO supportive housing facilities in New York, and on the basis of residents' feelings about their experience, both positive and negative, formulated a program. This program, and the accumulated knowledge of the nonprofit Corporation for Supportive Housing, guided the design of the prototype.

The residents wanted a place that would allow them to forget their housing past. "They wanted colors, décor, artwork, attractive furnishings and other enhancements to create a homelike, less institutional environment. It was important that the facility not 'look like a dump' or like any of the places where they had recently come from."[5] For example, although the size of an apartment is important to residents, simply making it larger is insufficient. What is more important is defining the spaces: if the residents cannot see the kitchen from the bed, or the bed from the door, then even a small unit will seem larger and more homelike. The prototype apartment, a mere 235 square feet in area, satisfies these preferences with a separate dining space so that residents and their guests will not feel as if they are eating in the bedroom (figures 44 and 45).[6]

The architects, Gran-Sultan Associates, developed units, combinations of units, plans for services and other shared spaces, and then whole building designs. Documentation in the manual explains the reasoning behind the design decisions and how each element satisfies the program requirements. The units' floor plan incorporates an important feature that architects try to achieve in all housing: a sense of transition from public to private spaces. Small apartments, and particularly studios, often fail to provide transitions within the space; the threshold is undifferentiated from the main space. Although the kitchenette of the Gran-Sultan prototype apartment is situated in the entry (which doubles as the dining area), the space still feels like a vestibule serving the remainder of the dwelling. This thoughtful planning is carried through into the prototype's common areas. The design specifies the location of shared areas within the facility, how each receives natural light and is open to other spaces (including outdoor patios), and how they can accommodate a range of activities. The architects then organized what they call the "kit of parts"—the individual program spaces—into schematic plans. To facilitate wide use of these plans, the architects created a series of schematic building designs for different types of lots in different contexts (figure 46). These include a corner building, a mid-block building, and buildings for a variety of densities. The ultimate test of a prototype, of course, is a real project; on the basis of the program and the prototype, architect Warren Gran built four SROs, each responding differently to site context, land conditions (such as topography and soils), and the preferences of the particular sponsor. In one building, the case-manager suite is adjacent to the public areas in order to encourage interaction while ensuring security; in another, the case-manager suite is farther removed from the public areas and an office is situated adjacent. Some buildings are larger than the initial prototype in order to amortize the higher site costs over more units.

According to Gran, the application of the prototype in the initial buildings like the Ivan Shapiro House (figure 47) worked well, but each sponsor operates its program differently, leading to variations in the design and more specific architectural input. The residents are staying longer than expected, making the SROs permanent rather than transitional housing.[7]

FIGURE 46 The supportive housing prototype can be adapted to different types of sites, including corners and midblock locations.

ENTRY AND LOBBY

In permanent supportive housing the transition from the street to the dwelling is treated differently than it is in shelters. A lobby or a shared living room, often monitored by a member of the staff who oversees this room and the entry, plays an important role in housing for the recently homeless. Most homeless people have lost their network of friends and family and their connection to a community. Once they leave the shelter or transitional housing and move into their own place, they run the risk of growing isolated; the risk is particularly acute for seniors, who often lack the ability to move about the city to connect with friends. The building is their sole domain. The common area is a place to be with others and to entertain people outside the confines of their small unit.

The public areas of this housing may include a dining room. People may choose to cook for them-

FIGURE 47 The Ivan Shapiro House in Manhattan by Warren Gran is based on his supportive housing prototype.

selves if their room is equipped with a small kitchen, but communal meals provide an opportunity to form ties with others, and they provide some assurance of a well-balanced, professionally prepared diet.

Ideally the lobby and the dining space are open and connected to one another, viewable by an individual who serves as doorman and security guard. This person monitors the space but also serves the more important function of screening those who arrive. One of the benefits to residents of such housing is the sense of security—an assurance that they were denied when living on the streets; here, they have a protected home and a protector. This is not to say that residents cannot have guests, only that the guests must be invited and monitored, since they might be former associates who are still homeless, or using drugs or alcohol. Sometimes guests are not allowed beyond the monitored public areas. Assurances of supervision, tight management, and that rules will be enforced can be valuable as well in mitigating neighbors' objections to the facility.

These new SROs are often considered permanent housing, but they do not look like houses. It may be that so long as the detached house is viewed as the preferred form of housing in the United States, anything else will seem substandard. My intent in designing multifamily housing is to incorporate as many features of the single-family house as possible. One important element of this program is that a unit be perceived as an individual unit even when it is combined with many other dwellings. An SRO, however, does not easily lend itself to this treatment. Perhaps it could if the concept of an individual dwelling were to yield to the notion of the large, shared residence. This concept underlies many of the grand apartment buildings that surround Central Park in New York City. The cachet of living in the venerable Dakota or the San Remo is comparable in urban areas to the individual mansion on an estate. On a much more modest scale, an SRO, particularly one with a prominent front door, a lobby, and security, can provide the same sense of home for those who were once homeless or living in a shelter.

Even within shelters, having a personal space that militates against its context—a facility that is shared with many other people—can evoke the same powerful associations of individuality, security, and territoriality that define the idea of "home." This remains the most important program requirement, for it is home, after all, that the homeless are seeking.

DESIGN 5

THE FIRST-CENTURY B.C. Roman architect and writer Vitruvius described the objectives of architecture as *firmitas, utilitas,* and *venustas:* firmness (structure), commodity (function), and delight: a building must be structurally stable, it must satisfy the functions required of it, and it must inspire. One would hope that all buildings satisfy the first two objectives, but it is capacity to delight that distinguishes "architecture" from mere "building."

Historically, public housing in the United States has tended to concentrate on function at the expense of permanence and the capacity to give its residents pleasure. During the last two decades, however, these stark, repetitious, and uninspiring structures have given way to significant architecture. When the federal government abandoned housing subsidies in the 1970s, nonprofit organizations known as community development corporations (CDCs) stepped in to subsidize the construction of low-income housing The emphasis that the CDCs placed on good design gave these nonprofits credibility in their communities and leverage in the increasingly competitive funding arena. Most important, it helped them fulfill their mission—to house people with low incomes in a dignified manner, setting a standard for the thousands of nonprofit developers that now build affordable housing throughout the country.[1]

Architects, who in the past had tended to ignore housing as a building type, were now called upon to focus their talents on designing affordable housing for nonprofit developers. These architects and their CDC clients, recognizing the mistakes of the past, resolved not to repeat them. "The projects"—large boxlike buildings placed on vast expanses of cleared land—were no longer viable. Rather, new affordable housing would be low-rise and medium-density, and it would fit into communities, rather than stand apart from them.

We must go a step further now: to do for homeless housing what we have been doing during the last two decades for other types of affordable housing. Nowhere are firmness, commodity, and delight more important than for those whose lives have had so little of each. The discussion that follows examines some examples of projects created specifically for homeless populations in cities throughout the United States to show how architects approach these design challenges.

In the previous chapter I discussed the functional considerations that guide the design of housing for the homeless. Emergency, transitional, or permanent housing for the homeless cannot exist without associated support facilities, and each group of occupants has specific needs and requirements. A building that houses individuals with chronic diseases, for example, will be different from a building intended for individuals seeking refuge from an abusive spouse. Building codes and health department regulations help ensure that what we build is safe. The site of the building, whether it is a renovation or a new structure, and often the sources of the funding determine its form (and make boilerplate solutions unfeasible). These considerations guide the housing's *utilitas* and *firmitas*. But what about *venustas*—the delight?

Architects derive inspiration from different sources. Sometimes the program and circumstances are so circumscribed that the architect must search within them to find the clues that reveal the delight. This is the case, for example, when the program is the preservation of a historic structure. In other instances, the architect's empathy for the residents—the profound insight—is the starting point. Often architects begin by asking questions: "What should this place be?" "What should it represent?" "What will make it special?" Often the answer is a metaphor.

Contra Costa County Adult Shelter
Concord, California
Davis & Joyce Architects

When I began the design for the expansion and renovation of the Contra Costa County Adult Shelter I felt that the prospect of injecting delight into a facility that was so deeply flawed was an impossible task. Nevertheless, I fought the urge to deal exclusively with firmness and commodity. The facility occupies a former warehouse in an industrial area near a freeway, isolated from the commercial and residential sections of the city of Concord, a middle-class suburb of San Francisco. The one-story structure, converted several years earlier into a temporary makeshift shelter, had become a permanent facility, even though it lacked appropriate spaces for clients and staff, proper ventilation, and adequate bathrooms.

The shelter as I found it brought to sickly life the metaphor of warehousing the poor. I realized that there was a more hopeful metaphor inherent in the building's desolate setting that could motivate its design. Like other industrial sites, the shelter's setting was full of discarded building material that had begun to pile up and deteriorate. I decided to make use of this palette of materials: to transpose and recombine them into a functional building design that would offer the shelter's residents and staff both utility and beauty. I carefully selected materials like those found near the shelter's building—wood, corrugated metal, cement panels—using them in an architecture that created a whole more significant than its individual parts or materials. I see this transformation as a positive metaphor for the residents of the

FIGURE 48 The wood, metal, and cement materials that form the structures within the building's shell are similar to those found discarded in the vicinity of the Contra Costa County Adult Shelter.

shelter: they reconstruct lives that are in disarray, through the interventions of the staff, in a safe, protected environment. The re-created warehouse would help the shelter's residents re-create their lives.

The concrete shell of the warehouse is hard, intractable, and keeps out the elements. I viewed it as a boundary within which to build a separate world, an interior made up of buildings within a building. Each small building houses elements of the shelter's functions—offices for counseling, bathrooms and showers, and classrooms—and their sequence forms an enclosed streetscape along which residents travel (figure 48). On one side, the space between the new small buildings and the existing shell is a public area: a plaza for residents, staff, and guests (figure 49); the space on the other sides is divided into private areas, containing dormitories for men, women, and special-needs clients (figure 50).

The shelter was originally lit exclusively by bare fluorescent bulbs mounted near the eighteen-foot-high ceiling, which consists of exposed foil-backed insulation. No funds were available to cover or replace the ceiling, but the ambient lighting in the public activity spaces was improved by substituting smaller, inexpensive industrial fixtures. Streetscape-style lighting, mounted at intervals along the sequence of small buildings, softened the effect of their warehouse context. The openings at two sets of large roll-up doors were glazed to bring daylight into the otherwise windowless building; interior triangular courtyards facing these windows provide the residents with a protected space with a view to the outdoors. The renovated shelter, with its increased capacity and newly created program spaces, has evolved from an emergency shelter to a transitional facility. Residents stay up to ninety days, during which time they attend classes held in one of the new interior "buildings," or undertake culinary training in the facility's new commercial kitchen.

The redesign of the Contra Costa County Adult Shelter has provided the facility with greater flexibility to meet the needs of homeless men and women; it has done so by transforming a warehouse into a welcoming, safe, and comfortable physical environment in which its residents can stabilize and transform their lives.

FIGURE 49 The plaza area inside the Contra Costa County Adult Shelter.

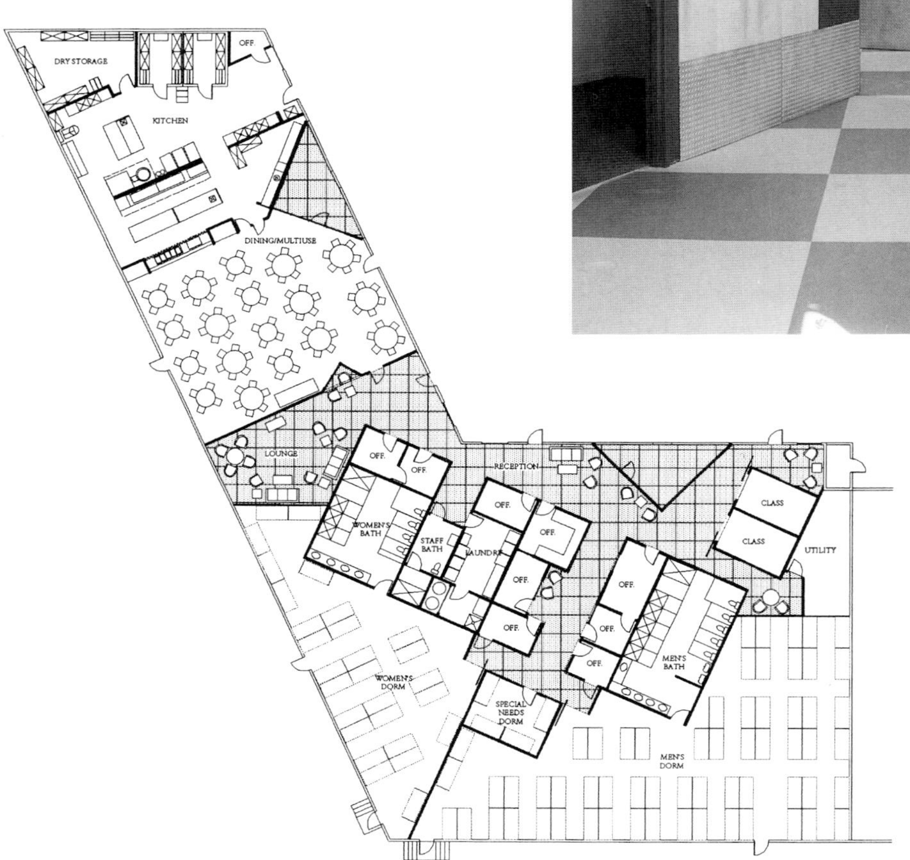

FIGURE 50 The structures within the warehouse of the Contra Costa County Adult Shelter separate the public areas from the sleeping areas and house the enlarged bathrooms, as well as specialized program elements such as classrooms and offices.

FIGURE 51 The architects used the image of an ark as a basis for the design of the Salvation Army's Center of Hope shelter in New Orleans.

Salvation Army Center of Hope
New Orleans, Louisiana
Errol Barron

When Errol Barron was commissioned by the Salvation Army to design a shelter in New Orleans, his original design used elements associated with domestic architecture—dormers, a pitched roof, and intimate spaces—to define its physical structure. But the complexity of the shelter's program, which needed to accommodate 260 people (some housed in dormitories, others in apartments), and included large dining facilities and a variety of social services, made the house analogy impractical.[2] The small architectural gestures would have added to the cost without advancing the shelter's function. Budget and durability were more important to the client than the small-scale domestic elements that Barron had originally proposed.

The shelter was to be situated in a middle-class residential community next to a medical center. Abandoning the conception of the Center of Hope as a house, Barron began to explore elements that the proposed facility and its neighbor held in common: well-being and health. These characteristics favored the use of durable institutional materials and required a plan more efficient than the intricate residential form that Barron had originally proposed. The reconception of the facility as a health-related facility rather than as a homeless shelter, moreover, made its presence more acceptable to residents of the neighborhood.

Barron devised the metaphor of an ark to guide the facility's design (figure 51). "We thought of it less as a home and a bit more as a vessel, or sanctuary, where people could go and make a retreat from the 'troubled waters' around them."[3] Barron's revision of the Center of Hope's design expresses the metaphor in materials and form: the

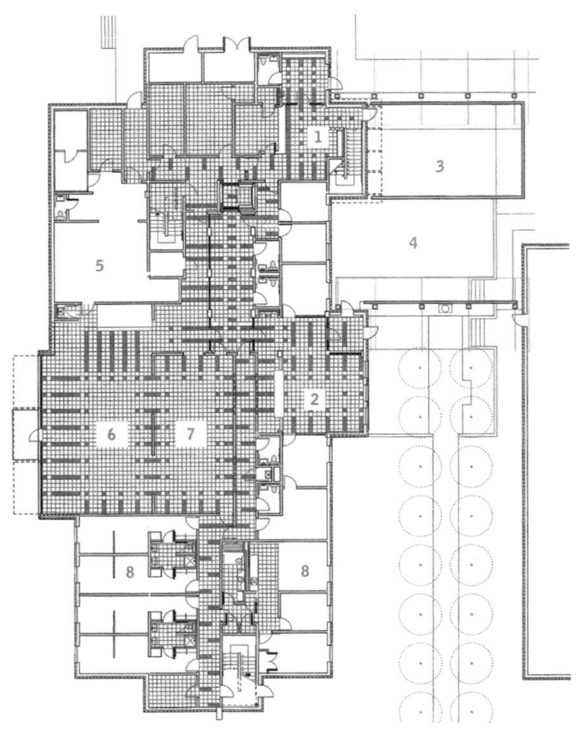

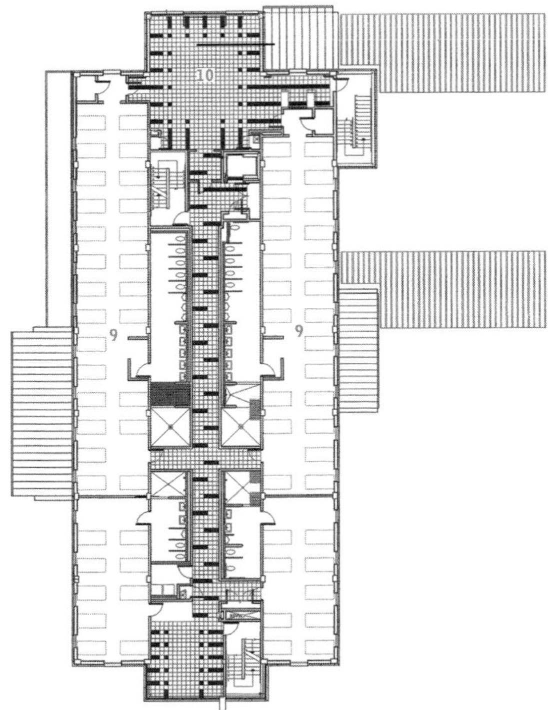

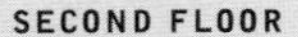

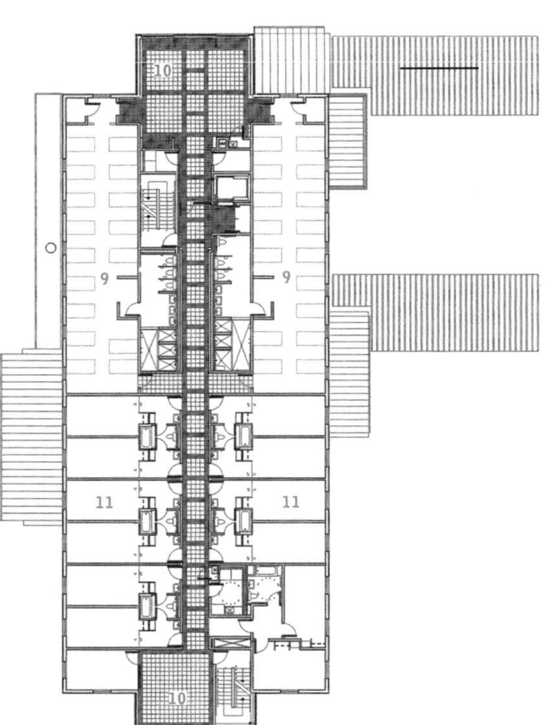

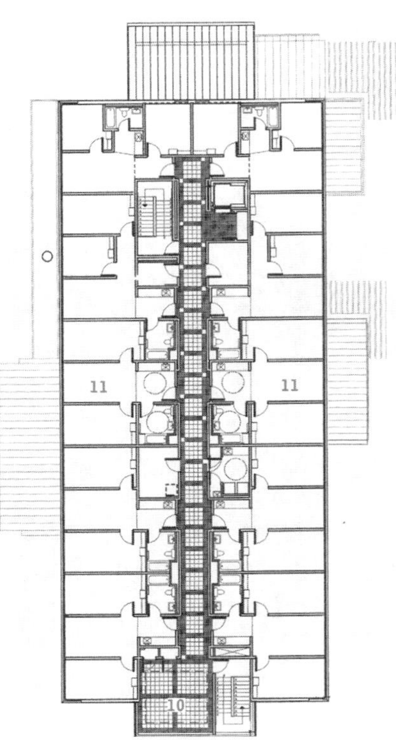

FIGURE 52 Plans of the Salvation Army's Center of Hope.

KEY

1 Men's entry
2 Women's entry
3 Men's smoking courtyard
4 Women's smoking courtyard
5 Kitchen
6 Dining room
7 Meeting room
8 Apartment
9 Dormitory
10 Library/lounge
11 Bedroom

lower floor is brick and more solid in appearance than the floors above, like the hull of a ship. The center's common spaces, situated at the ends of the building on a residential floor, are wrapped in glass, resembling a ship's bridge.

Programmatic issues also informed the shelter's design, in particular concerns among the facility's neighbors that the long lines of those waiting admission would spill into the community. For that reason, the entries are placed along the back, away from the street. Men and women have separate lobbies, and they reside on different floors. Most of the residents are accommodated in dormitory spaces, but private bedrooms are available to women and children who are victims of domestic violence. The top floor is composed of transitional housing apartments for families, who can stay here for up to six months (figure 52).

Barron intended the metaphor of the ark, manifested in the building's shape and materials, to suggest sanctuary in a "subliminal but in some ways precise" way.[4] The metaphor, like the analogy of a mission used for the Joan Kroc Center of the St. Vincent de Paul Village in San Diego, is a particularly apt strategy for injecting delight into shelters sponsored by religious service organizations.

Assisted Care and After Care Facility
Larkin Street Youth Services
San Francisco, California
Davis & Joyce Architects

When I began to design the nation's first housing for homeless young people with HIV/AIDS, I asked some of the facility's anticipated residents what they wanted the building to be; they told me only what they *didn't* want: an institution. The antithesis of an institution is a house. Although the existing building and urban setting didn't lend themselves to a design based on residential architecture, I nevertheless began by thinking about how a large family might live together: How and where would they interact? Where would they go to be alone? How would they greet and entertain guests?

In the late 1980s, Larkin Street Youth Services, which has been serving homeless youth in San Francisco since 1981, began to see a large increase in HIV-positive clients, reflecting a relatively new hazard associated with intravenous drug use and high-risk sexual behavior among young people living on the street. The medication protocols for treating HIV and AIDS in the early 1990s, comprising a large number of drugs that had to be taken at specific times during the day, required a high level of discipline. Since many of these young people lived on the street or were housed by the center in residential hotels, the counselors and medical staff of Larkin Street Youth Services were unable to ensure that their clients were taking the medications as directed. The center needed a means of housing its HIV/AIDS clients in an environment that removed them from the hazards of life on the street and in which their activities and their health could be closely monitored.

The facility's design needed to meet very specific criteria, both to accommodate the needs of this particular group of residents and to satisfy the requirements of the various funding sources, such as the San Francisco Department of Public Health, which has specific regulations regarding medical clinics and food service. It was assumed, for example, that residents would become incapacitated at some point, so the entire building had to be designed to accommodate disabilities. The building was intended to be a home for the center's clients, but it was also intended as a school, a medical clinic, and in some cases a hospice. Larkin Street Youth Services had devised a two-part program for assisting HIV-positive homeless youth: (1) permanent supportive housing for twelve young people, each with a private room and bath; and (2) other

FIGURE 53 Plans of the Assisted Care and After Care Facility of Larkin Street Youth Services. The courtyard in the middle brings light into the long, narrow structure and provides a protected outdoor area for activities.

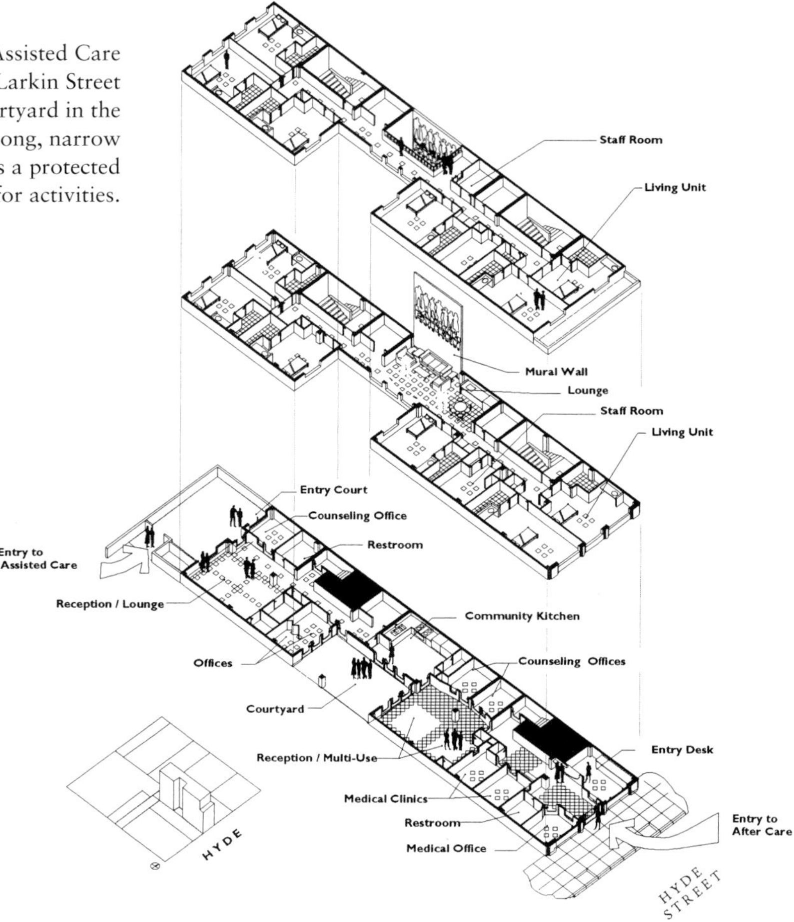

spaces that would make the facility a home for its clients, including living rooms, counseling spaces, a kitchen, and a dining room. The permanent residents share some facilities with other young people (many of them also HIV-positive) residing outside of the facility, often in nearby rented hotel rooms. Both permanent residents and those living elsewhere share regular meals at the facility; they attend classes and group sessions together, and they have equal access to a medical clinic, but these shared facilities were funded separately and therefore had to be distinguished from the permanent supportive housing in the building plan, even though all those served by the facility would in fact be using the public spaces.

Other elements of the program, however, were less formally defined. Many of the drug protocols for treating HIV and AIDS were ineffective or experimental when the project was initiated. We had to anticipate that many of the residents would become weakened or disabled from the effects of the illness or the medications. Could the type, size, and configuration of the facility's spaces be designed to accommodate future disabilities? Might certain colors be psychologically beneficial? In the absence of effective medical treatment for AIDS at the time, it was assumed that some residents would die, so we needed to create a design that would moderate the trauma of these deaths on other residents.

The Larkin Street Assisted Care and After Care Facility was to occupy an existing building in San Francisco's Tenderloin, an area that in other cities would be known as skid row. Contained in an Art Deco historic zone, the building had a certain charm, but it also had many deficiencies, not the least of which was a concrete structure that did not meet the city's stringent seismic codes and required extensive and expensive retrofitting. The building's site is long and narrow, which made the placement of individual living units difficult, and the building itself was far too small for the center's range of programs. Adding a floor was a obvious means to enlarge the space, but the city's policy on historic buildings prohibited alterations to the facade: the added third floor was therefore set back so that it would not be visible from the street in front of the building.

Adding a courtyard at the center of the building resolved several programmatic and logistical issues. Each of the twelve bedrooms had to have a window for light and ventilation, a need that was not problematic for the two bedrooms facing the street and the two bedrooms facing the alley in back, but had to be accommodated in bedrooms at the interior. Piercing a courtyard into the building made it possible to bring air and light into interior bedrooms on the second floor and the new third floor (figure 53). The courtyard is the focus of the building, providing an outdoor alternative to the street for residents, who use it as a smoking lounge (all the residents seem to smoke). This satisfied area merchants who were concerned about vagrancy, but it also protected the residents and made it possible for staff to monitor them.

The courtyard is an extension of the main shared public room on the ground floor, as well as the adjacent kitchen (figure 54). This arrangement is both symbolic and functional. I had hoped that the facility's twelve permanent residents would socialize with those coming to the building for meals and clinic services: these public spaces provide an area for these exchanges. The residents also have separate lounge areas, one in the rear of the building and a smaller unit upstairs among the private bedrooms; at the same time that it brings the center's constituencies together, the courtyard thus separates private areas used exclusively by the residents from those shared by young people coming for counseling, clinic services, and meals. As it turned out, the users of the facility form a tight subculture in the city; there was therefore no need for a common living-room space at the ground floor, so the room is now used as a teaching and meeting space.

The building's medical clinic, used by residents and other Larkin Street clients, is situated on the building's first floor, facing Hyde Street. The clinic's design was guided by the assumption that clients would want privacy, and thus concentrates the medical and counseling offices in one location in order to avoid the need to move through the building and encounter other clients and visitors; even the waiting area is somewhat hidden behind a column (figure 55). The placement of the clinic allows a single staff member to monitor the front door and handle intake.

The top two floors are the residents' private domain, but I was concerned that those on the third floor might be isolated from the others and from the public functions on the entry level. To ensure a visual and psychological connection between the residents of the two floors, I placed a two-story

FIGURE 54 The contiguous lounge, courtyard, and kitchen (not shown) are the focus for the public functions of the Larkin Street Youth Center's Assisted Care and After Care Facility.

lounge on the second floor that can be viewed from the passageway above, forming a second internal courtyard that connects the two residential floors. The lounge, at the center of the building, receives natural light from the adjacent exterior courtyard and a skylight. The corridor on the third floor forms a bridge in the middle of the building, with a view to the lounge on one side and to the courtyard on the other. Opening the middle of the building thus brought light and air into the structure, while enabling staff to monitor activities throughout the building, discreetly but effectively.

The plan of the Larkin Street Assisted Care and After Care Facility is much like that of a large house, with a public foyer area at the entrance (where visitors are greeted), and a residential area made private by limiting visual and physical access. The common living spaces— kitchen, dining room, and parlor—occupy the middle of the ground floor, while the private bedrooms are situated on the floors above. Social exchanges take place throughout the building: residents visit each other in the bedrooms and small groups meet in the second-floor lounge, as well as in public areas within the building.

From the perspective of current and former residents, the design seems to have satisfied our objectives and assumptions. Residents value the facility's homelike ambience, although some take exception to the some of the bright colors in the

FIGURE 55 The reception lobby of the Assisted Care and After Care Facility of the Larkin Street Youth Center.

private spaces (many find yellow, in particular, too bright and unsettling). As in other group homes, cliques have formed, and the residents' experience of life on the streets has not been entirely overcome: the television and VCR in the upstairs lounge were stolen and have not been replaced. But improvements in the treatment of AIDS and conditions associated with HIV, as well as the stable living environment, have fortunately challenged some of our expectations about the facility. The residents are remarkably healthy given their HIV status; none of the more disabling conditions that we anticipated has developed, and none of the residents has died. With their health improved, the residents of the assisted care facility at the Larkin Street Youth Center are finding jobs, and they are choosing to move on to permanent housing, generally within a year of their admission.

PATH—People Assisting the Homeless
Regional Homeless Center
Los Angeles, California
Jeffrey M. Kalban & Associates

A shopping mall might seem an unusual and even insensitive model for the provision of services to the homeless, but People Assisting the Homeless (PATH), a Los Angeles nonprofit, saw value in consolidating social service programs in a single location, both for those needing services and for those providing them.

FIGURE 56 The mall of the PATH regional facility concentrates social services in a single location.

Private and governmental organizations that work with the homeless are often criticized for failing to coordinate their efforts. Although computerized tracking of benefit recipients has, in principle, helped make the system more efficient, this means little to individuals obligated to shuttle from one area of town to another to receive care; often they simply give up. In fact, finding an appropriate location for PATH was problematic, as there is a substantial homeless population both in the downtown's skid row and in West Hollywood, and a great distance between the two. PATH selected a site equidistant between the two areas, accessible from either by bus.

The PATH mall brings together nineteen different agencies in a single regional facility (figure 56). The anchor tenant, in the parlance of the commercial mall, is the resource office, situated near the entry. Homeless clients in need of mental health counseling, for example, are directed from a reception desk (which doubles as a security station) to an agency within the facility; other services include substance abuse counseling, the Salvation Army, travelers' aid (to assist those seeking a return home), and a beauty parlor (figure 57). There is also an office of the Los Angeles Superior Court. Here the service provider can privately check the status of outstanding warrants of a client seeking services, and then assist in adjudicating the matter in the courthouse, which is also in the mall.

The space is wide, tall, and well lit. Each of the service spaces has a glass storefront, giving the

FIGURE 57 Plans of the PATH regional facility. The mall and administrative offices are located on the lower level; housing is located on the upper floors.

FIRST FLOOR

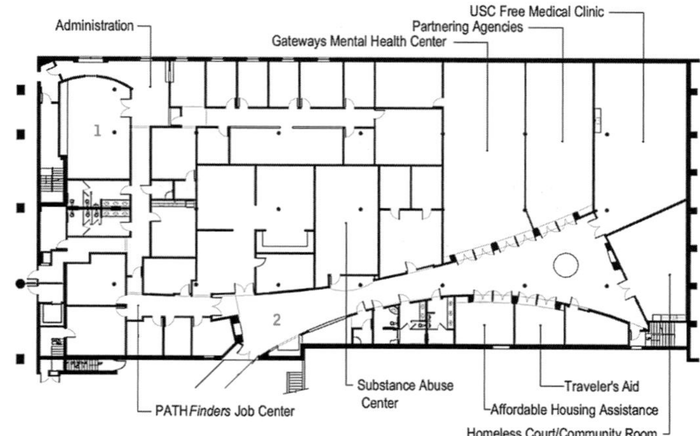

KEY

1 Conference
2 Mall
3 Play yard
4 Kitchen
5 Living/dining
6 Kids' study
7 Lounge
8 Library
9 Dining/recreation
10 Women's shower
11 Women's dorm
12 Lobby
13 Reception
14 Men's shower
15 Men's dorm

SECOND FLOOR-WOMEN'S

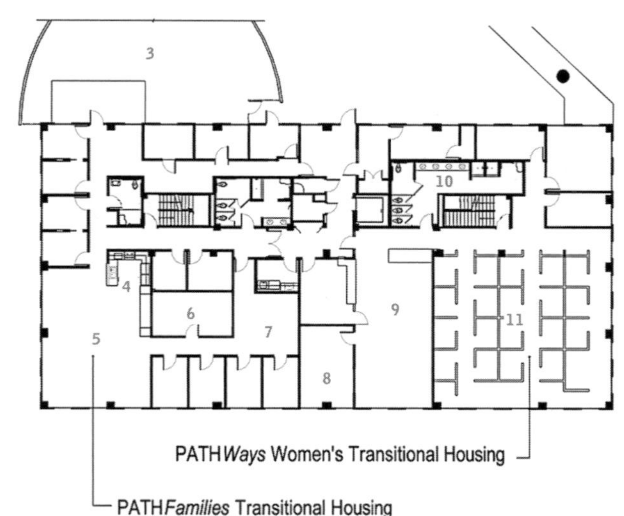

THIRD FLOOR-MEN'S

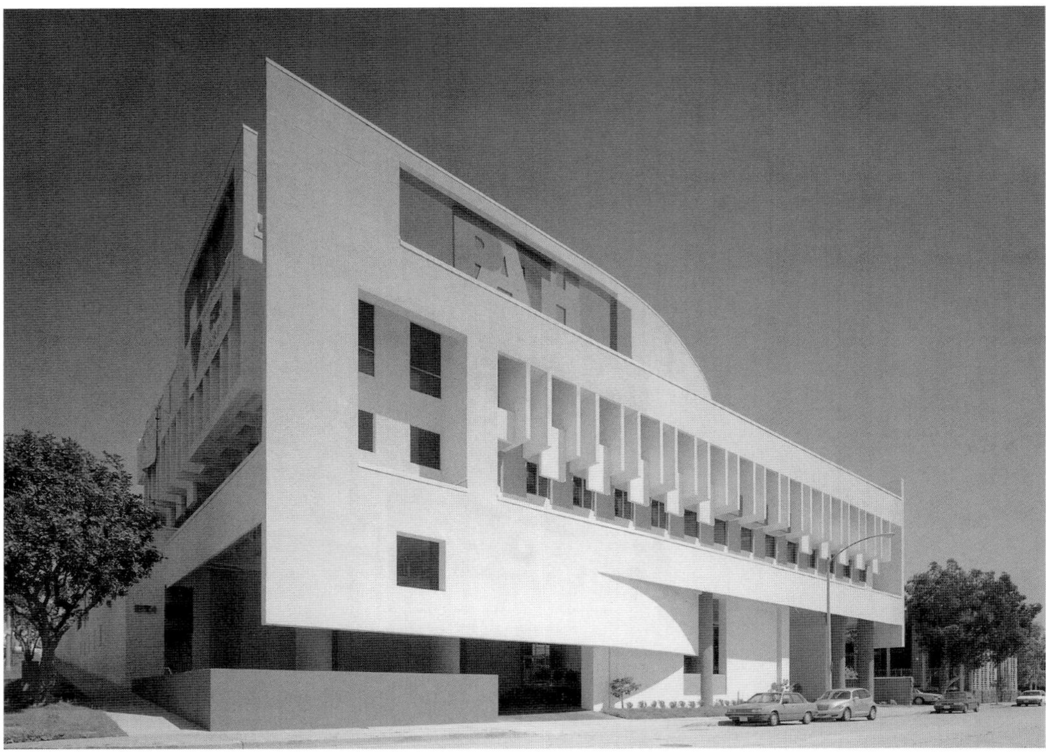

FIGURE 58 The PATH regional facility in Los Angeles is a converted printing plant. Its bold forms and colors are easily visible from the neighboring freeway.

mall a lively and accessible character. One of the advantages of this design is that upon arriving, a person can look into the spaces, see others receiving assistance, and be an observer before becoming a participant. The mall is a fitting analogy not just because of its convenience to the clients, but because it is a culturally familiar environment that reinforces the notion that the homeless have choices.

Although the mall element has been the object of particular attention, the PATH facility includes housing services as well, which are distinguished from the mall by a separate entrance (figure 58). Some of the living quarters are reserved for families, who, once accepted for admission, may stay in the facility for up to five months on condition that they save 80 percent of their income in lieu of paying rent (residents are required to find employment within thirty days of their admission). The facility includes separate temporary housing for those with HIV/AIDS, and a three-bed emergency overnight shelter for walk-ins or homeless individuals brought in by the police. PATH intends to build permanent housing as well on areas of the site currently used as a parking lot: the facility, when complete, will thus offer a complete range of services and housing to its clients.

PATH's temporary housing for families includes several innovative design elements. Private rooms are separated by sliding doors so that the spaces can be configured to accommodate large and small families, and corridors that link the rooms have small alcoves fitted with benches. These are intended for reading to a child while another child sleeps within the private room. A large multipurpose room includes a kitchen, which is shared among several families since the rooms do not include cooking facilities; an adjacent space is used in the evenings as a teaching space for adults, enclosed in glass so that parents and children can see one another. Just outside this area is a rooftop play yard, accessible only from the living quarters as a security measure.

The PATH facility is a secondary use, converted from a large abandoned printing plant by the architect Jeffrey Kalban, whose buildings reflect his interest in the fine arts, including sculpture and painting.[5] The facility, which combines the bold sculptural forms of the original structure with bright primary colors, is a powerful collage visible from some distance, as well as from the freeway that runs alongside it. Unlike other urban homeless facilities, which must often contend with opposition from the community and thus seek to make their presence unobtrusive, the PATH facility's industrial location has given it the relative freedom to advertise itself visually.

This exuberant image coincides with the analogy of a commercial mall, which seeks high visibility and immediate recognition. Like affordable housing in general, this approach walks a delicate line. Is the facility seen as a progressive and accessible place that fulfills a social obligation, or does it further stigmatize the homeless population by drawing additional attention to them? The PATH regional facility makes a good case for the former. The message here is that programs for the homeless are taking place in well-designed buildings and that vibrant architecture is part of the solution.

Canon Barcus Community House
San Francisco, California
Herman and Coliver

The starting points for the buildings described above were metaphors and analogies, abstract ways of thinking about design to guide decisions and give rise to insights about what the places might be. Another approach is that of "first principles" and "profound insights." A profound insight is often a set of statements about how people will live in a place and what features will support that lifestyle. Each design decision is then tested against these statements.

The Canon Barcus Community House in San Francisco, designed by Herman and Coliver for Episcopal Community Services, is supportive housing for homeless families, including families transferring from other shelters and transitional housing, living on the street or in cars, or occupying SROs. The architects' insights regarding this population cluster around connections—the residents' connection to the immediate neighborhood, and the connection of residents to one another. The connection to the neighborhood provides a sense of belonging and stability for the homeless, who have little sense of community. The architects placed the shared facilities at ground level, with views to and from the sidewalk. This visual access creates a connection between the residents and the neighborhood; architecturally, it gives something to the neighborhood by creating an interesting street-level facade that reveals activity within (figure 59). The portion of the building that contains job-training classrooms is two stories high, located on the corner, with its own entry. Individuals from the community using these programs have easy and clear access; those living in the building

FIGURE 59 The Canon Barcus Community House. The housing is situated above the street-level community services.

enter the job-training facility from within the housing.

A separate, prominent entry for the housing—marked by an awning, glass doors, and a recess—is also an important element of the building's design. It signals that this is a real home, with long-term residents, and a permanent part of the community. The Canon Barcus Community House also makes a connection to the larger community in a way that has less to do with the specific residents and more to do with its environment: a city with a strong architectural character. It is a prototypical mixed-use city building, based on the tradition of living above street-level shops. In this case the shops are not retail establishments but centers that provide social services. Each unit within the housing above has a bay window. The windows enliven the facade, and they reduce the apparent size of the large block that the building occupies, but they also reveal that the building is composed of individual residential units—that this is a home to many people.

Connecting the residents to one other is equally important, particularly when so many are single parents with children. The children have the opportunity to forge friendships, and parents (many of whom are employed) have the opportunity to

FIGURE 60 One of the courtyards of the Canon Barcus Community House. A bridge connects two buildings and spans a lower-level day care play yard.

share child-care responsibilities. Among the architectural features that encourage this connection are corridors that resemble porches, facilitating chance meetings. These corridors open onto three separate courtyards (figure 60), bringing natural light into the passageways and providing views into the activity spaces. The architects anticipated that the courtyards would be play areas; providing multiple courtyards gives residents choices and at the same time reduces the concentration of children (and thus noise) in any one space.

The site is T-shaped, comprising two buildings: a long one facing the street, and a smaller one in back. Between the two is the largest of the open spaces, which occupies two levels (figures 61 and 62). On the first level above the street, the plaza

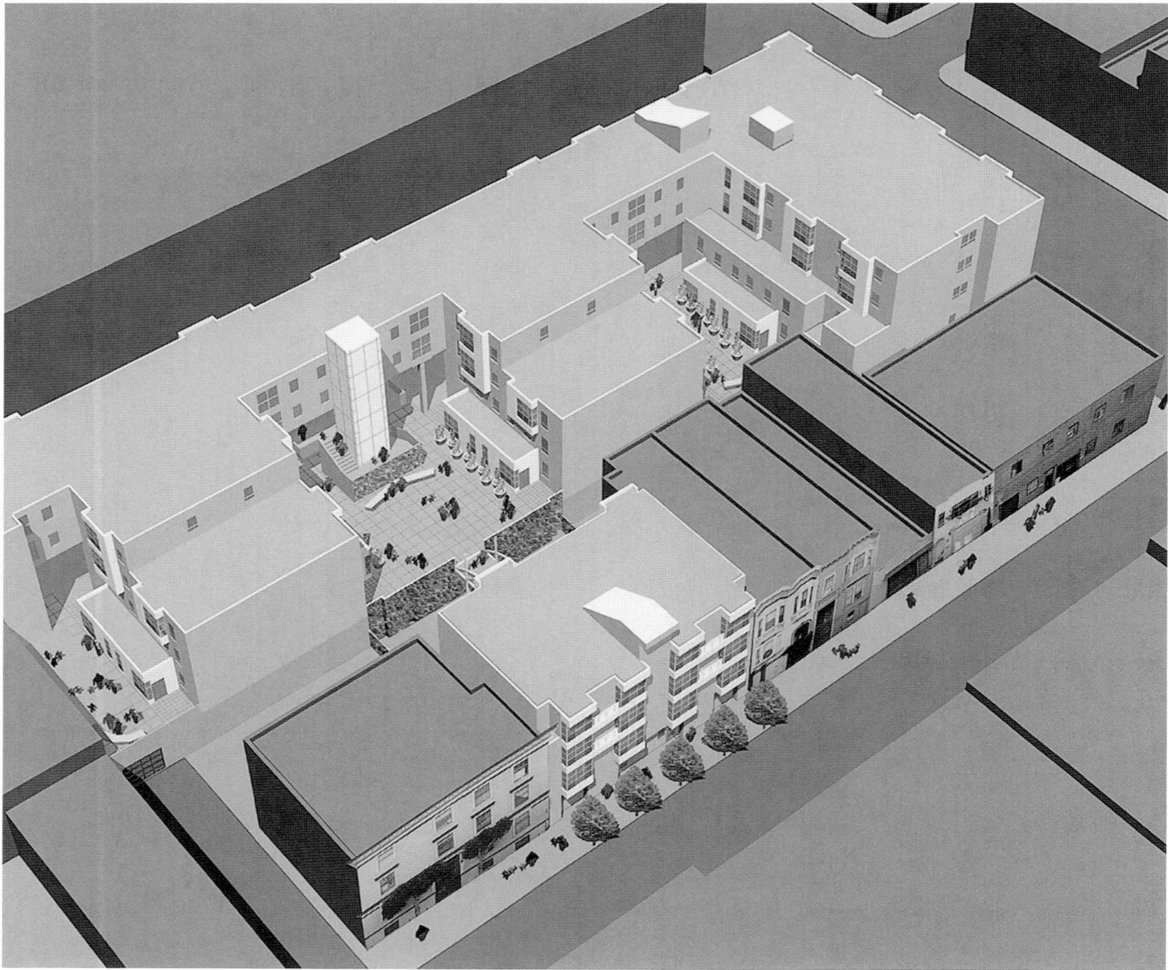

FIGURE 61 Three separate courtyards are linked by a system of corridors. Each provides an activity space for the many resident children of different ages.

serves as an extension of the hallway that is adjacent to a shared lounge. The townhouse-type dwellings are entered from this space, which is the focus of the complex, defining it as a communal space. At the ground level, and visible from the court above, is the on-site day care play area.

The site is small and irregularly shaped, the program ambitious, and the logistics of managing both left a narrow range of design approaches. Nevertheless each building element—a hallway, an entry, an open space—is transformed by the architects' special insights about the residents and their needs. The rudiments of function are elevated to features of delight.

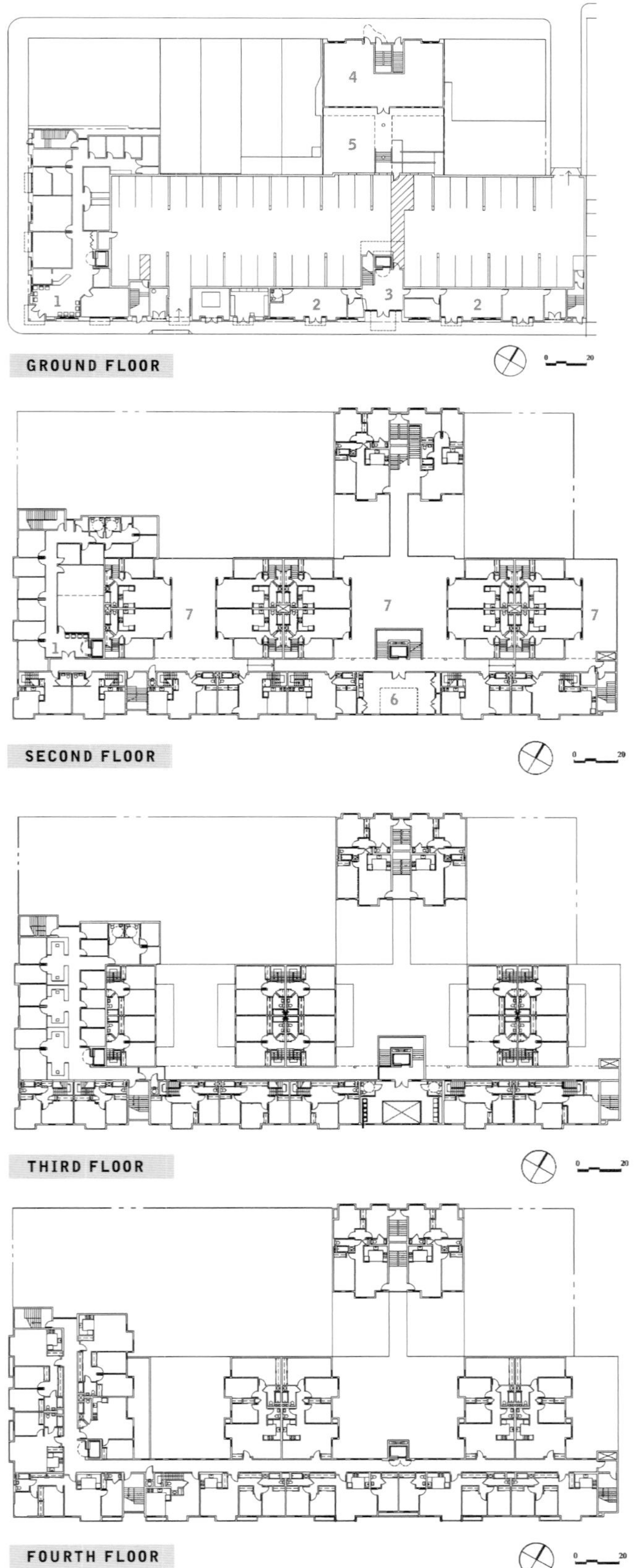

FIGURE 62 The plans of the Canon Barcus Community House. Townhouses are entered from the second-level courtyard. Most of the hallways are single-loaded, with units on only one side.

KEY

1 Social services
2 Staff offices
3 Residents' offices
4 Daycare
5 Daycare courtyard
6 Community room
7 Residential courtyard

Transitional Housing for the Homeless
New York City
Skidmore, Owings & Merrill

The projects described in the previous discussion are unique. They were designed for specific sites or in existing buildings, and for particular service providers with highly defined programs. But what if the objective is to build several projects simultaneously when neither the sites nor detailed programs have yet been identified?

One solution is to design a set of components and develop guidelines and instructions showing how the components could be arranged. This is the kit-of-parts approach used by Gran-Sultan discussed in the previous chapter. The prototype does not anticipate every situation and context, and therefore needs to be interpreted and applied to specific circumstances. This flexibility allows the architect of each building to draw inspiration from the location and circumstances, but it also necessitates unique buildings and requires a commitment of time and money to design them. There is little of the potential cost advantage of replicating similar buildings and constructing them simultaneously.

New York City began to develop transitional housing in the late 1980s in response to the ruling in *Callahan vs. Carey* that required the city to provide accommodation for anyone seeking shelter. The city commissioned two types of facilities, one for single adults and the other for families with children. The goal was to build a total of twenty facilities, each intended to house between two hundred and fifty and three hundred people. Skidmore, Owings & Merrill (SOM), one of the nation's oldest, largest, and most highly regarded architectural firms, was retained to design prototypes and then set them on sites throughout the city. The firm was known primarily for designing skyscrapers, not for its work in affordable housing or social services–related enterprises; its ability to design institutional buildings of high quality within a budget and to manage large building projects efficiently made SOM a sensible choice for a project that demanded both. These qualities, as well as the firm's offer to undertake the project at its own cost, without profit, led to SOM's selection.

SOM's strategy was to create a set of repeating "house" components comprising several units each, and then connect these components in ways that would fit various site configurations.[6] The firm's prototype design for the family transitional housing comprises two unit types: studios, and double units whose kitchen and dining space are shared by two families (figures 63 and 64). These are intended to enable single-parent families to share household responsibilities (including child care), and thereby encourage a sense of community. These double units with a common kitchen worried some city officials who were uncertain whether the sharing would work, but they have proved very successful. The two types of units are assembled in wings, each with a central stair and a large common area; a clerestory brings natural light into the interior (see figure 63). The common area was intended to define smaller neighborhoods within the complex and to provide space for programs. The building is entered through a pavilion with offices on the ground floor and additional common rooms above, and the pavilion links to the wings by corridors (see figure 64).

The housing for single adults clusters the bedrooms into "houses" of eight rooms that share a kitchen, two bathrooms, and a two-story living room (figure 65). These shared kitchens, however, have not been successful. The eight individuals sharing a "house" do not always form a congenial family, owing to differences in eating habits and daily schedules, and differing abilities to

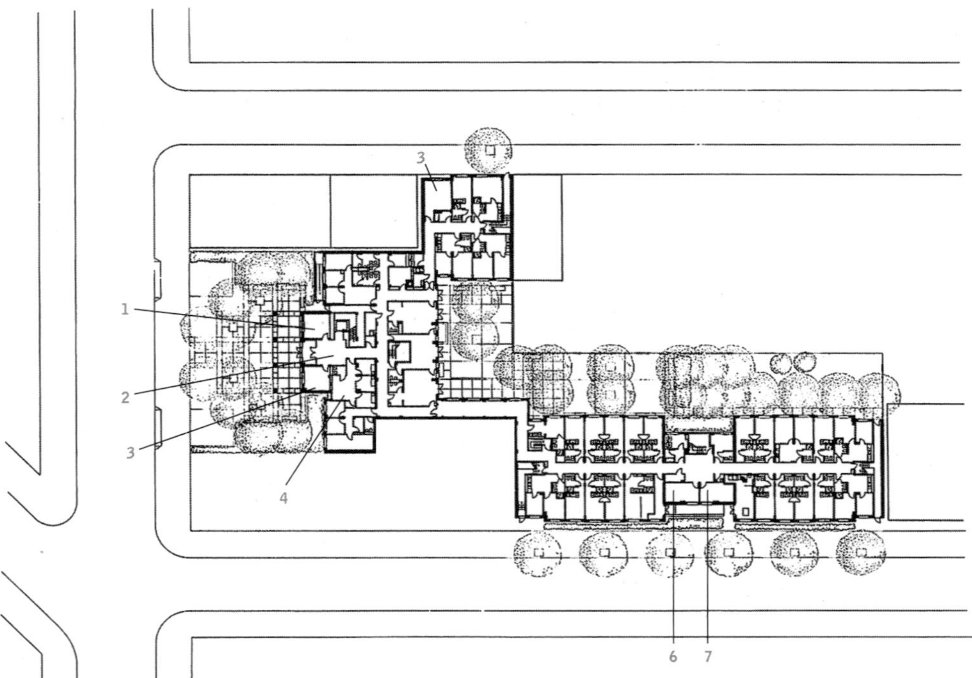

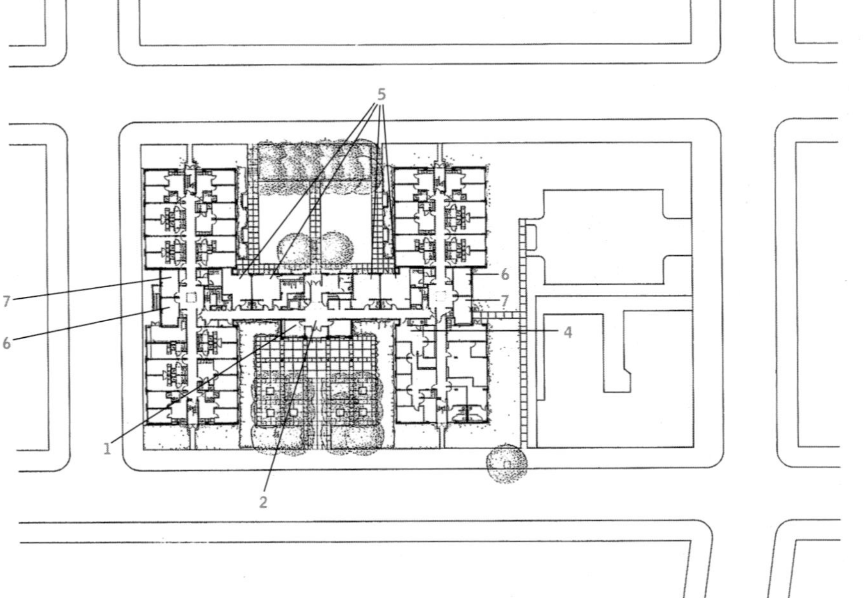

FIGURE 63 Prototype plans for New York City's family transitional shelters.

KEY
1 Office
2 Lobby
3 Lounge
4 Medical
5 Childcare
6 Quiet area
7 TV

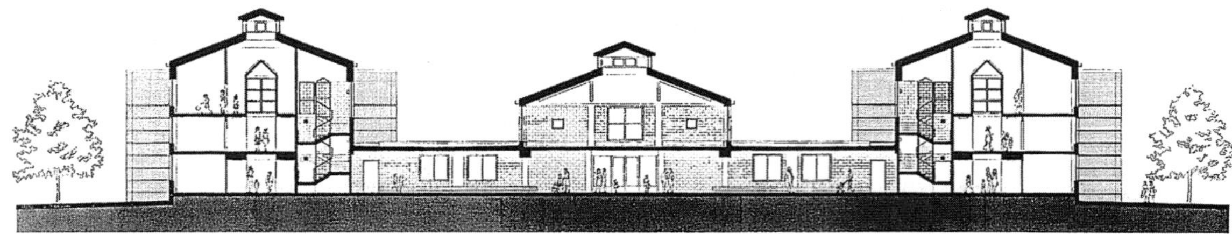

FIGURE 64 A section of a prototype of New York City's family transitional shelters shows the entry pavilion (center) with an activity space on the second level. This building component is linked by a corridor to residential wings.

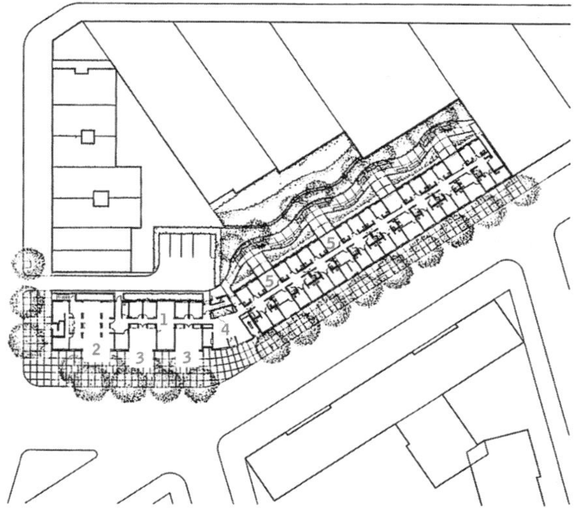

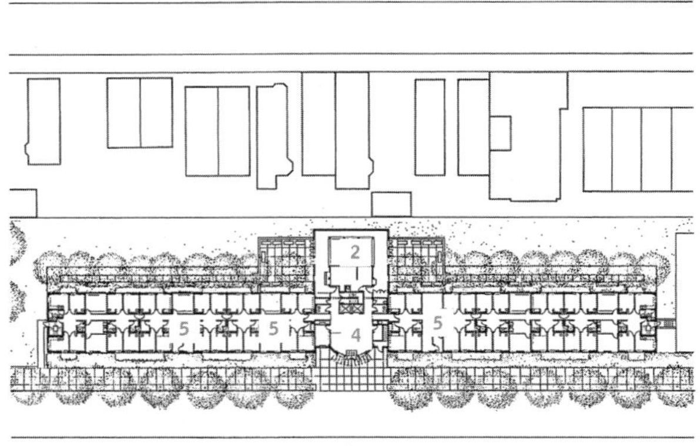

FIGURE 65 Prototype plans for New York City's transitional shelters for single adults.

KEY

1 Administration
2 Dining room
3 Meeting room
4 Lobby
5 Lounge

collaborate with many others. The lounges associated with each house have been converted from informal communal rooms into program space. As with the kitchens, the groups are not sufficiently compatible or capable of sharing. Furthermore, as the city transferred the operation of these facilities to service providers funded by the city, each has established specific programs for residents that were not originally anticipated and required additional space.

The brick buildings are sturdy and well made with consistent detailing (figures 66 and 67). The costs of construction were reduced by replicating fabrication details and materials, but since the buildings are constructed to an institutional standard comparable to that of prisons, they were still

FIGURE 66 A Family Transitional Shelter. Nine shelters were built throughout New York City on the basis of the prototypes designed by Skidmore, Owings & Merrill. The architects placed a premium on durability in these modern, well-detailed structures.

quite expensive.[7] In each prototype, the buildings' architectural diversity is concentrated in the public spaces or in the connections between the wings and houses. The two-story lounge areas in the single-adult building, for example, bring natural light into the corridors. On one floor the lounge is contiguous with the corridor; windows create views through the lounge to the outside. Windows in the upper portion of these two-story volumes bring light into the upper corridor. Relief from the long corridors is provided by recurrent views through other spaces and by natural light (figure 68). These prototypes were built on several sites throughout New York City's boroughs. The sites were quite different from one another, and although the designs were based on similar elements and principles, each prototype facility had to be adjusted to fit its location.

A decade after their construction, the New York City transitional facilities remain in use and are in reasonably good condition, a testament to the durability of the constriction and selection of materials. Only nine of the projected twenty facilities were ultimately built, primarily because of the difficulty of finding sites that did not raise community objections to the permanent presence of the homeless. Some view these unobtrusive buildings as respectable, well built, and appropriate,[8] but

FIGURE 67 One of the transitional shelters for single adults. The two-story common areas are emphasized along the facade.

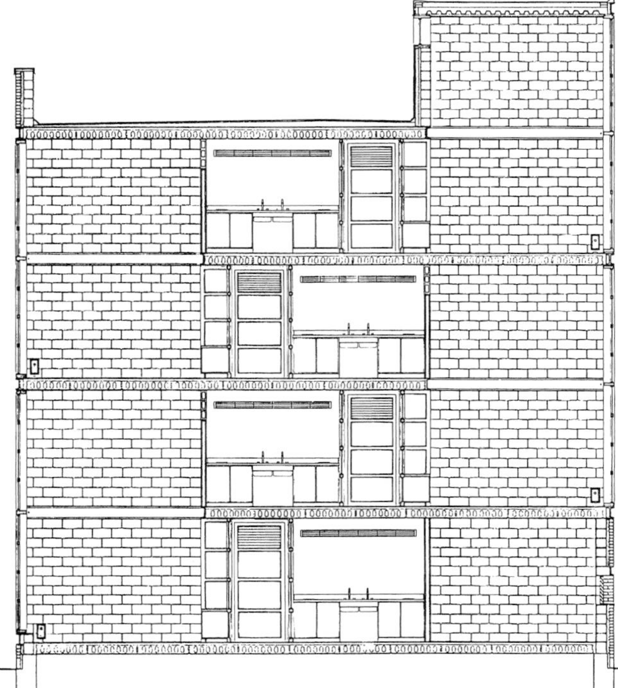

FIGURE 68 Two-story lounges along the corridors provide views into the activity areas and natural light for the halls.

their austere modernism has also been criticized as joyless and institutional.[9]

Designing affordable housing requires balancing construction efficiency and the uniqueness that a specific site, program, and preferences of the service provider and the residents demand. This balance is particularly hard to achieve using the prototype approach. Overemphasize building efficiency and you can end up with a rudimentary shelter that pleases neither the neighbors nor the residents. Accentuate the uniqueness of the circumstances and you risk higher costs and accommodate fewer homeless. I believe that SOM achieved a proper balance, particularly in the prototype for families, by using some of the architectural strategies discussed in the previous chapter. Segmenting the housing components into smaller groupings reduces the scale of the buildings, enabling them to fit more discreetly into neighborhoods. The smaller housing components benefit the residents by making a large complex seem much smaller. By bringing natural light into the interiors the architects were able enliven spaces, particularly the corridors. And in both prototypes the informal communal spaces along the corridors, although no longer used for their initial purpose, nonetheless provide variety, views, and choices for the residents.

The Prince George Hotel
New York City
Beyer Blinder Belle

As an architectural monument, the Prince George Hotel in New York City was so far gone that many had given up hope of its resurrection. But the Prince George, like the Contra Costa Adult Shelter, is a metaphor of the people who now live there. They needed some attention, some respect, and a bit of professional help to reveal their attributes. Seeing this potential behind its dilapidated state, Common Ground, a nonprofit developer of housing for the homeless, embarked on converting the venerable structure into permanent housing for low-income homeless people and people with HIV/AIDS. It did so by taking advantage of tax credits granted for renovating historic structures in order to finance a significant portion of the cost.

The Prince George was built in 1901 on East Twenty-eighth Street as a luxury hotel; its lobby at the time was larger than any in New York City, and the adjacent ballroom once called to mind the grand ocean liners of the early twentieth century. By the 1980s, however, the Prince George had entirely lost its allure; it was a notoriously grim welfare hotel, with the dubious distinction of being the largest homeless shelter in the United States, housing as many as sixteen hundred people, including many children. Crime and prostitution were rampant in the building to such an extent that resident children could guide visitors through the halls, pointing out rooms used for smoking crack and others used for shooting heroin.[10] By the late 1990s, the conditions had grown so abhorrent that the shelter was closed and the Prince George vacated.

The building nonetheless had many features that made it appropriate as housing for homeless or low-income residents, including 493 rooms that could be reconfigured and refitted into single-occupancy units with small kitchens, a grand lobby at street level, and several large spaces that could be used as offices and social services. The program elements necessary for larger facilities could easily be accommodated within the building. Its mid-town location meant that residents had easy access to public transportation, jobs, and other services. There was the added advantage that this elegant structure, once restored, would have a grandeur that would make any resident proud (figures 69 and 70).

FIGURE 69 The floor plans of the Prince George Hotel *(here and opposite)*.

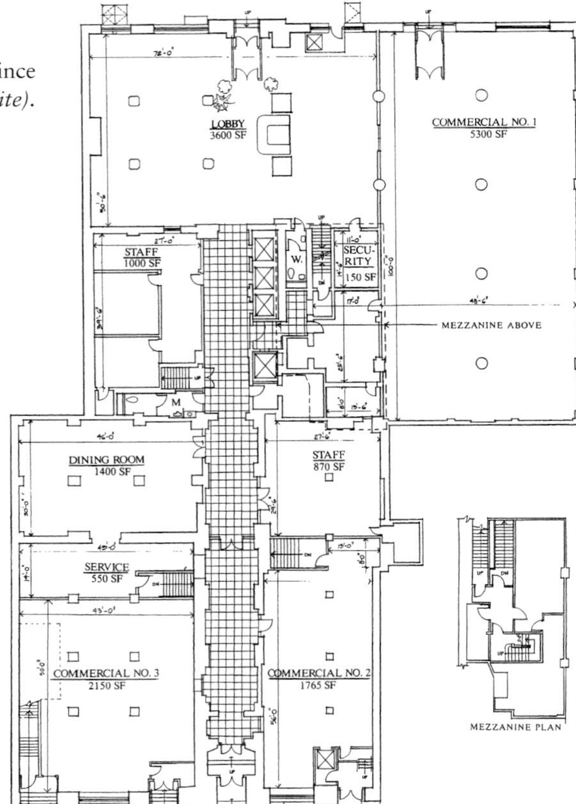

FIGURE 70 The facade of the Prince George Hotel, in New York City. By the 1990s, the once-elegant hotel had become a notorious homeless shelter. Restored to its original elegance, the hotel has been converted into apartments for the homeless.

Although the building was structurally sound and of a size that accorded with its intended use and program, much of the infrastructure (including plumbing, electrical wiring, and ventilation) needed replacement; the Art Deco elements that distinguished its interior architecture required extensive restoration (figures 71–73).[11] In all, the renovation and restoration cost $40 million, raised through a combination of ten different city, state, and federal programs and private institutions. The building's operation is supported by a combination of subsidies, from seven different agencies and organizations, and rent (equivalent to 30 percent of income) paid by the residents.

The critical elements seemed to be in place: a suitable structure, good location, available funding, and a nonprofit developer willing to take on the challenge, but the intent to house a population that was low income, formerly homeless, and/or HIV-positive met with heated opposition in the community. A local real estate broker spoke for many when he said that "the idea they are going to be involved in this at my expense and limit my ability to make a living by their presence is nauseating."[12] These objections were overcome to some extent by Common Ground's recent success in converting the Times Square Hotel, once known as "Homeless Hell," into a permanent low-income housing and services facility. The project was also helped by hiring the prominent architectural firm of Beyer Blinder Belle, well known for its historic preservation work at Grand Central Station and Ellis Island.

FIGURE 71 The lobby of the Prince George Hotel before renovation.

FIGURE 72 The lobby of the Prince George Hotel after renovation.

FIGURE 73 A detail of the wall and decorative molding in the lobby of the renovated Prince George.

New York City mayor Rudolph Giuliani also supported the project. Common Ground's commitment to supportive housing and to careful tenant screening also went a long way toward alleviating community concerns, and the local community board voted overwhelmingly in favor of the rehabilitation of the hotel. These commitments include 24-hour security, on-site counseling, health services, and job training. Those with substance abuse problems are not accepted, nor are individuals deemed unable to live independently. To demonstrate its commitment to the project, Common Ground moved its administrative offices into the top floor of the Prince George.

When the Prince George was formally opened in early 2000, there were four times as many applicants as dwellings. The facility has lived up to its promise. The public areas are open, inviting, beautifully detailed, and impeccably maintained. The 416 individual studio units, reduced from the original 493 to allow for a communal room on each floor and other office and program space, are clean and well appointed (figures 74 and 75). Like the building itself, the residents have the opportunity to renew themselves as an integral part of their community.

Using metaphors and analogies to articulate their vision, the designers of these places sought

FIGURE 74 A bedroom in the Prince George Hotel, illustrated here prior to renovation, is now a studio apartment.

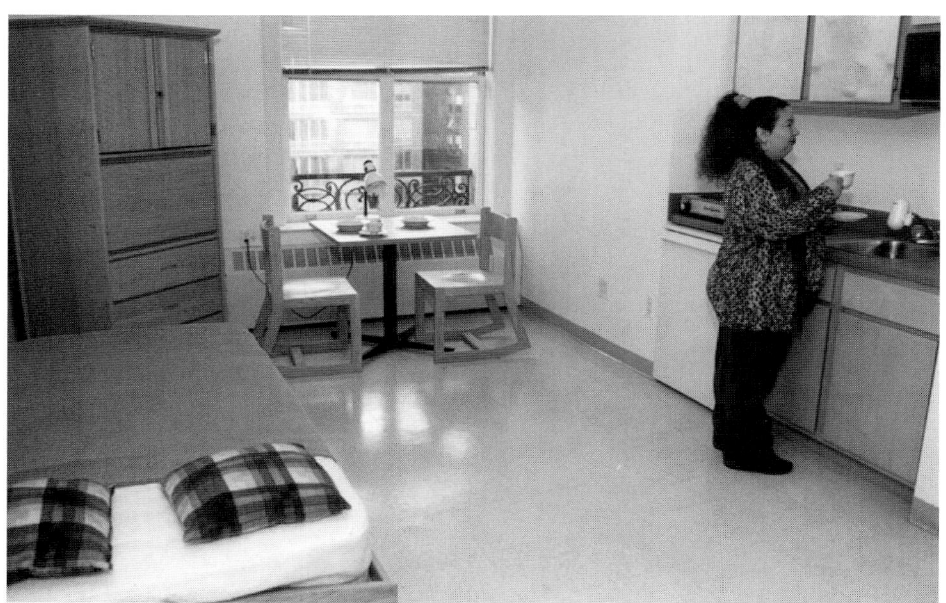

FIGURE 75 A newly refurbished studio at the Prince George.

to find delight hidden within the program, an insight revealed through an understanding of the residents, or by taking inspiration from an existing structure. Each strives to make a large facility seem smaller—by clustering elements and linking them, by placing smaller components within larger volumes, or by creating courtyards. These strategies help accommodate as many people as possible on a scale that seems less overwhelming and institutional than the alternative. Particular attention to color and material selection is an important consideration that links these project—the combination of common materials in the Contra Costa County Adult Shelter, the sturdy and well-detailed masonry and glass of SOM's New York housing, the refurbishment of decorative embellishments in the Prince George Hotel. The attention to the visual and textural qualities of a space add delight.

Even with these commonalities, the results of the projects are completely different from one another, reflecting the diversity of the homeless populations served, the unique circumstance of each project, and the variety of architectural approaches that designers can use in housing the homeless.

AFTERWORD

THIS BOOK HAS FOCUSED on the contributions that architecture can make in overcoming homelessness. Some examples, like the St. Vincent de Paul Village in San Diego, are large and ambitious. Others are small gestures—the design of a personalized cabinet for use in a shelter or the reconfiguration of a dormitory space to provide the occupants with increased privacy and feelings of control. A recurrent theme throughout this book has been that we need to make the most of modest budgets, but to do so in a way that sustains the dignity of those who reside in these spaces. We must strike a balance between efficiency and vitality, between commodity and delight. No magic formula can provide these facilities quickly and inexpensively. The building techniques and architectural devices that we use in designing other types of housing—natural light, variations within spaces, color, and visual access to the outdoors—must also be employed in housing for the homeless.

Two themes predominate. The first is that homeless people are not a homogeneous population; the profile of homelessness includes men, women, and an increasing number of children; it includes the young and the old, the employed and the unemployed, individuals who are in relatively good health and individuals with a variety of physical and mental health problems. Understanding this diversity and applying this knowledge to our designs is critical to the success of our buildings. Designs for homeless youth with HIV/AIDS will be different from those for single adults with mental health problems. Facilities for families with children will be different from those for seniors. The second theme is that housing alone is insufficient. The inclusion of social services tailored to the needs of residents is necessary if we are to address the full range of underlying causes of homelessness. Throughout the entire continuum of care, from emergency shelter to permanent residences, supportive housing has to be part of our designs.

We have also seen that any architecture for the homeless will have several clients. One goal is to reintegrate the homeless into our communities; in doing so we must ensure that the facilities built will be accepted by their neighbors. Sometimes this will require rejuvenating buildings that were once prominent in the community, like the Prince George. We can also create new buildings like the Canon Barcus Community House that make use of materials, scale, and form to fit comfortably within their neighborhoods. The focus on housing with support services also demands that we consider those who work with the homeless. One role of architecture is to mediate between the often conflicting needs of those who occupy our buildings. In shelters, this requires providing for both the privacy of residents and the ability of staff to monitor activity. In permanent housing, it entails providing for the residents' independent living, while encouraging communal activity and connections to support services so they do not become isolated.

The examples in this book are evidence that successful designs for the homeless can be achieved when the client and architect strive to exceed the basic need of rudimentary shelter. Those who work with the homeless are committed to their mission; architects need to gain inspiration from this commitment, conceiving these projects not only as socially responsible practice but also as intellectually challenging and creative endeavors.

Many architects with whom I spoke while conducting research for this book had not intended to specialize in this particular subfield of architecture; in accepting their first project to design housing for the homeless, they initially viewed it as just another commission. Often their participation was fortuitous: a friend or acquaintance serving on the board of a homeless service organization simply approached them and asked them for help. Many of these architects, however, have been drawn more deeply into services for the homeless as a result—sometimes as designers specializing in emergency, transitional, or permanent housing, but sometimes also as consultants, as members of nonprofit boards, or as advocates for the homeless.

My own involvement in designing facilities for the homeless grew out of my interest in housing: I began my career working with market-rate housing developers, moved into working with nonprofit organizations that sponsor affordable housing, and in the 1990s, found myself designing housing for the homeless. It is the most challenging yet rewarding work that I have ever done. Riding down the elevator one day with the contractor in a renovation I had designed to transform a large emergency shelter into a transitional facility, a resident asked us if we were involved in the work under way. We said yes, and braced ourselves for the certain earful that we would get for all the disruption. His reply surprised us: he said that no one had ever designed anything for him before, and he thanked us for our efforts in making his life better.

Architects shouldn't wait for the call. Many homeless service providers can use their help today—even if it amounts to no more than a few hours of consultation. Every community has organizations working with the homeless, and almost all of these organizations work in venues that need physical improvement. Not all architects will necessarily want to devote their time exclusively to designing housing for the homeless. But all architects *can* play an important role by supporting those who do: by attending public hearings and speaking up for projects, by helping to raise money for their construction, and by encouraging young architects in their firms to volunteer their time and expertise.

We also need to see the positive aspects of these efforts. Media accounts about homelessness tend to concentrate exclusively on the increasing numbers of homeless people and the plight of individuals. Although these serve an important function in informing the public about a phenomenon that is easily overlooked, the media themselves often tend to overlook the stories that demonstrate workable solutions: the successes, the humanitarian organizations, the new buildings, and the individuals who have been helped by these efforts. Architectural journals similarly need to promote the profession's sense of social responsibility in creating housing for the homeless and to reinforce the message that this is a field in which architects can make a difference.

The phenomenon of homelessness has so many elements that it will take a combination of solutions (and the efforts of many) to alleviate it—a commitment comparable to our national efforts to fight diseases like cancer. Like the treatment of cancer, the treatment of homelessness is not satisfied by a single approach: different forms of homelessness respond differently to different treatments; progress tends to be incremental, and early detection is critical. The most effective way to treat homelessness is by enabling those at risk to avoid it, but homelessness is a reactive phenomenon that can be exacerbated by seemingly unrelated events or apparently innocuous decisions. Some policymakers, for example, have recently considered releasing aging prisoners whose health is failing on the grounds that they are no longer a threat to society and that the cost of incarcerating and caring for them is high. If we do not create supportive housing for them, where will these individuals go, and how will they receive medical attention? Many will likely become homeless. At the other end of the spectrum are the young: at the age of eighteen, boys in shelters are deemed adults and are separated from their mothers and younger siblings. In the absence of facilities for this cohort, they are cast into adult shelters or onto the street. They lose the last vestige of a protected social unit—the family—and they become increasingly vulnerable to drugs, crime, and long-term homelessness.

The examples throughout this book are but a few in what is now a growing national enterprise in cities all around the United States: architecture for the homeless. Each represents an incremental step toward a cure. These projects, most of which were created within the last decade, are testament to the fact that architecture is, by definition, about designing accommodation and that well-planned buildings constitute a critical element of meeting the challenge of housing the homeless in a dignified manner. My hope is that that our society is now ready to redirect public and private resources to this important social undertaking.

NOTES

PREFACE

1. Social Science Data Analysis Network, "Census 2000—California Population Growth," Censusscope 2000, http://www.censusscope.org/aboutCensus2000.html.

INTRODUCTION

1. Robert C. Coates, *A Street Is Not a Home: Solving America's Homeless Dilemma* (Buffalo, N.Y.: Prometheus Books, 1990), chap. 10.

2. Deborah K. Dietsch, "Shelter from the Storm," *Architectural Record* 174, no. 6 (1986): 136–42.

3. Interview with Father Joe Carroll, San Diego, November 8, 2002.

4. Ibid.

1 WHOSE PROBLEM IS IT?

1. National Alliance to End Homelessness, "A Plan, Not a Dream: How to End Homelessness in Ten Years," http://www.endhomelessness.org.

2. National Coalition for the Homeless, "Fact Sheet 2" (February 1999), http://www.nationalhomeless.org.

3. John M. Glionna, "Squalor amid the Glitter," *Los Angeles Times,* December 28, 2001.

4. Heidi Sommer, "Homelessness in Urban America: A Review of the Literature," paper read at Urban Homelessness and Public Policy Solutions: A One-Day Conference, January 22, 2001, Institute of Governmental Studies—the Richard and Rhoda Goldman School of Public Policy and the University of California Program of Housing and Urban Policy. Estimates of the U.S. Conference of Mayors are based on responses to its surveys; the National Survey of Homeless Assistance Providers and Clients bases its data on reports from its members about the number of individuals who have used services. Other sources and studies are summarized in Sommer, "Homelessness in Urban America."

5. U.S. Conference of Mayors, *Annual Survey,* 1998. The survey reports that 67 percent of homeless families are single-parent households.

6. U.S. Conference of Mayors, *Annual Survey,* 2002.

7. Chicago Metropolis 2020, "Recommendations for Developing Attainable Workforce Housing in the Chicago Region" (Chicago: Chicago Metropolis 2020, 2002); Vince Hoenigman, "Homelessness in a Progressive City" (San Francisco: San Francisco Planning and Urban Research Association, August 2002).

8. National Survey of Homeless Assistance Providers and Clients, "Demographic Characteris-

tics of Homeless Clients, " in *Homelessness: Programs and the People They Serve* (Washington, D.C.: National Survey of Homeless Assistance Providers and Clients, 2002). The NSHAPC survey estimated that the elderly constitute 8 percent of the homeless nationally. Hoenigman ("Homelessness in a Progressive City") found that they constitute 20 percent of the homeless in San Francisco.

9. James D. Wright, Beth A. Rubin, and Joel A. Devine, *Beside the Golden Door: Policy, Politics, and the Homeless* (New York: Aldine de Gruyter, 1998), 21; National Coalition for the Homeless, "Questions and Answers about the Chronically Homeless Initiative," http://www.nationalhomeless.org/chronic/chronicqanda.html. Like counting the homeless in general, counting the chronically homeless—those with recurrent episodes of homelessness—is difficult. A federal government initiative to help the homeless is focused on 10 percent of all homeless, a target figure derived from an analysis of shelter requests in New York City and Philadelphia. Because only two metropolitan areas were surveyed, and because others have placed the number as high as 25 percent, however, the National Coalition for the Homeless feels that the program is insufficient to assist all those who are chronically homeless.

10. National Survey of Homeless Assistance Providers and Clients, "Demographic Characteristics of Homeless Clients." The survey estimates that 33 percent of all homeless men are veterans. Veterans constitute 31 percent of the nation's male population.

11. U.S. Conference of Mayors, *Annual Survey, 2001* (Washington, D.C.: U.S. Conference of Mayors, 2001). Figures vary widely by city. In Santa Monica, for example, the survey found that 56 percent of the homeless were mentally ill.

12. Ibid.

13. R. Fantasia and M. Isserman ("Homelessness: A Source Book," *Administration in Social Work* 20 [1996]: 97–98) estimate that as much as 18 percent of the rural population is homeless. The National Survey of Homeless Assistance Providers and Clients gives a figure of 9 percent in its 2002 survey. The disparity between the two estimates may reflect differing definitions of rural, suburban, and urban areas.

14. California Department of Housing and Community Development, "Raising the Roof: California Housing Development Projections and Constraints 1997–2020" (Sacramento: California Department of Housing and Community Development, 2000).

15. James D. Wright and Beth A. Rubin, "Is Homelessness a Housing Problem?" *Housing Policy Debate* 2, no. 3 (1991): 949.

16. Paul Groth, *Living Downtown* (Berkeley and Los Angeles: University of California Press, 1994), 9.

17. U.S. Department of Commerce, Census Bureau, Economics Statistics Administration, *Annual Survey of Manufacturers* (Washington, D.C.: Department of Commerce, Census Bureau, 2000), table 1; U.S. Department of Labor, Employment Standards Administration, Wage and Hour Division, "History of Federal Minimum Wages Rates under the Labor Standards Act, 1938–1996" (Washington, D.C.: Department of Labor, 2002).

18. Bernadette D. Proctor and Joseph Dalaker, *Current Population Reports: Poverty in the United States 2001* (Washington, D.C.: Census Bureau, 2001), 160–219.

19. Jennifer Wolch and Michael Dear, *Malign Neglect: Homelessness in an American City* (San Francisco: Jossey-Bass, 1993), 9.

20. U.S. Department of Health and Human Services, Human Services Administration, *Mental Health, United States, 2000* (Washington, D.C.:

Department of Health and Human Services, 2000), chap. 14.

21. Wright, Rubin, and Devine, *Beside the Golden Door,* 21.

22. Kim Hopper, "Public Shelter as 'a Hybrid Institution': Homeless Men in Historical Perspective," *Journal of Social Issues* 46, no. 4 (1990): 12–29.

23. Bobby Nell, quoted in Margie Chalofsky, Glem Finland, and Judy Wallace, *Changing Places: A Kid's View of Shelter Living* (Mt. Rainier, Md.: Gryphon House, 1990), 32.

24. Wayne, quoted in Chalofsky, Finland, and Wallace, *Changing Places,* 20.

25. Office of the President of the United States, *Fiscal Year 2002 Budget* (Washington, D.C.: U.S. Government Printing Office, 2002).

26. Martha R. Burt and others, *Homelessness: Programs and the People They Serve. Summary Report: Findings of the National Survey of Homeless Assistance Providers and Clients* (Washington, D.C.: Urban Institute, December 1999).

27. Coalition for the Homeless, "Rental Assistance for Working Homeless New Yorkers: A Cost-Effective Way to Reduce Shelter Capacity and Save Taxpayers Dollars," New York, Coalition for the Homeless, February 2001, http://www.coalitionforhomeless.org/downloads/rntalassistbriefpap2001.pdf.

28. D. P. Culhane, S. Metraux, and T. R. Hadley, "Public Service Reductions Associated with the Placement of Homeless People with Severe Mental Illness in Supportive Housing," *Housing Policy Debate* 13, no. 1 (2002): 107–63.

2 THE ARCHITECT AND HOMELESSNESS

1. Clare Cooper, *The House as Symbol of Self,* Working Paper 120 (University of California: Institute of Urban and Regional Development, 1971), 45.

2. Paul Groth, *Living Downtown* (Berkeley and Los Angeles: University of California Press, 1994).

3. Kim Hopper, "Public Shelter as 'a Hybrid Institution': Homeless Men in Historical Perspective," *Journal of Social Issues* 46, no. 4 (1990): 13–29.

4. Ibid., 16.

5. Peter H. Rossi, "Troubling Families: Family Homelessness in America," *American Behavioral Scientist* 37, no. 3 (1994): 365.

6. Elliot Liebbow, *Tell Them Who I Am: The Lives of Homeless Women* (New York: Penguin Books, 1993), 27.

7. James Wright, Beth Rubin, and Joel Devine, *Beside the Golden Door: Policy, Politics and the Homeless* (New York: Aldine de Gruyter, 1998), 15–21.

8. Interview with Sam Cobbs, Director of Program Services, Larkin Street Youth Services, San Francisco, February 28, 2002.

9. Interview with Brenda Springer, Public Relations Department, the Los Angeles Mission, Los Angeles, August 28, 2002.

10. Interview with Andy Lay, Chief Development Officer, the Union Rescue Mission, Los Angeles, August 28, 2002.

11. Telephone interviews with Scott MacGillvray and Herb Nadel, August 2002, respectively, architect of the Los Angeles Mission and architect of the Union Rescue Mission.

12. Groth, *Living Downtown,* 141.

13. David Isay and Stacy Abramson, with photographs by Harvey Wang, *Flophouse: Life on the Bowery* (New York: Random House, 2000), "Introduction."

14. Ibid., "Bobby Conners—Room 432."

15. Interview with Rosanne Haggerty, founder and Executive Director, Common Ground, New York, March 28, 2002.

16. Bettman/Corbis "Images of Home," *Metropolis,* April 2002, 34.

17. Ibid.

18. Ibid.

19. Paul Groth, presentation to graduate-level seminar on affordable housing, Department of Architecture, University of California, Berkeley, May 2001.

20. Interview, San Francisco, February 12, 2002.

21. The Tom Hom Group, "Campaige Place," Las Vegas, 2002, http://www.campaige.com.

22. Donald MacDonald, *Democratic Architecture: Practical Solutions to Today's Housing Crisis* (New York: Whitney Library of Design, 1996), 76.

23. Karen D. Stein, "Guerilla Welfare," *Architectural Record* 176, no. 11 (1988): 98.

24. Mark Lakeman, *Dignity Village: 2001 and Beyond* (Portland, Ore.: Dignity Village, 2001).

25. Interview with Ted Hayes, Los Angeles, August 28, 2002.

26. Carla Javits, "Building the Supportive Housing Movement," *Home Front* (summer 2002): 16.

3 SOME COSTS OF HOMELESSNESS

1. Patrick Hoge, "Squalor in the Streets," *San Francisco Chronicle,* November 4, 2001, and U.S. Conference of Mayors, "San Francisco: Creating Affordable Housing Opportunities in America's Most Expensive Housing Market," *U.S. Mayor Newspaper,* February 12, 2001, http://www.usmayors.org.

2. Patrick Markee, *Rental Assistance for Working Homeless New Yorkers: A Cost-Effective Way to Reduce Shelter Capacity and Save Taxpayer Dollars* (New York: Coalition for the Homeless, 2001).

3. Office of Policy Development Research, *Evaluation of the Emergency Shelter Grants Program,* 1: *Findings* (Washington, D.C.: U.S. Department of Housing and Urban Development, 1994).

4. Ilene Lelchuk, "Anger over Homeless Boosts Newsom," *San Francisco Chronicle,* August 6, 2002.

5. Donald A. Fox, "How Do You Spell Relief?" *San Francisco Chronicle,* July 26, 2002.

6. Kevin Fagan, "Urinetown: Not the Musical," *San Francisco Chronicle,* October 21, 2002.

7. Patrick Hoge, "Carted Away," *San Francisco Chronicle,* October 21, 2001.

8. Ibid.

9. Phillip Matier and Andrew Ross, "S.F. Activist Opens Tiny Door to Homeless," *San Francisco Chronicle,* September 25, 2002.

10. Kenneth R. Tremblay Jr., "Innovative Housing Solutions for Homelessness," *International Journal for Housing Science* 25, no. 1 (2001): 59–65.

11. Telephone interview with Chris Glaudel of Mercy Housing, July 3, 2003.

12. Sam Davis, "Why Affordable Housing Isn't," in *The Architecture of Affordable Housing* (Berkeley and Los Angeles: University of California Press, 1996), 63–81.

13. Telephone interview with Mark Gallen, West Regional Director for Construction for StayAmerica, August 8, 2002.

14. "Summary of Financial Feasibility Analysis," Berkeley, University of California, Office of

the President—Committee on Grounds and Buildings and the Committee on Finance, prepared for the University of California Housing Colloquium, University of California, San Diego, March 22, 1998.

15. Telephone interview with Randy Geer, construction administrator for the Oregon Department of Corrections, July 27, 2002. Minimum-security prisons have many collective programmatic features similar to those of homeless shelters, including sleeping wards, large dining facilities, and classrooms. The state of Oregon constructed several such facilities in the 1990s.

16. Interview with Robert McNeely, Vice President, Union Bank of California, June 26, 2002.

17. D. P. Culhane, S. Metraux, and T. R. Hadley, "Public Service Reductions Associated with the Placement of Homeless People with Severe Mental Illness in Supportive Housing," *Housing Policy Debate* 1, no. 13 (2002): 107–63.

18. Ibid.

19. Corporation for Supportive Housing, http://www.csh.org/ny.html.

20. Culhane, Metraux, and Hadley, "Public Service Reductions."

21. Student housing is subsidized through land costs (zero, since the land is already owned by the institution), and need-based scholarships most often cover room and board. Colleges and universities also benefit from state or federal underwriting of bonds to fund construction.

4 THE ARCHITECTURAL PROGRAM

1. Heidi Sommer, "Homelessness in Urban America: A Review of the Literature," paper read at Urban Homelessness and Public Policy Solutions: A One-Day Conference, January 22, 2001. Institute of Governmental Studies—the Richard and Rhoda Goldman School of Public Policy and the University of California Program of Housing and Urban Policy. Institute of Governmental Studies Press, Berkeley, California.

2. Interview with Joe Farro, Deputy Commissioner, New York City Department of Homeless Services, New York, March 28, 2002.

3. Chicago Metropolis 2020, "Recommendations for Developing Attainable Workforce Housing in the Chicago Region" (Chicago: Chicago Metropolis 2020, 2002).

4. Leslie Kaufman, "Shelters Seek to Oust Families Who Keep Rejecting Housing," *New York Times,* September 16, 2002.

5. Gran Sultan Associates, *Design Manual for Service-Enriched Single Room Occupancy* (New York: Corporation for Supportive Housing and New York State Office of Mental Health, Office of Housing Development, 1993).

6. Ibid.

7. Telephone interview with Warren Gran, November 12, 2002.

5 DESIGN

1. For a brief account of community development corporations, see Sam Davis, "The Architect and Affordable Housing," in *The Architecture of Affordable Housing* (Berkeley: University of California Press, 1996), 18–21.

2. Personal correspondence with Errol Barron, March 14, 2002.

3. Charles Linn, "Salvation Army Center of Hope," *Architectural Record* 185, no. 12 (1997): 68–69.

4. Baron correspondence, 2002.

5. Hugh Hart, "Built for Body and Soul," *Los Angeles Times,* March 4, 2002.

6. Personal correspondence with Skidmore, Owings and Merrill, February 26, 2002.
7. Interview with Joe Farro, Deputy Commissioner, New York City Department of Homeless Services, New York, March 28, 2002.
8. Eve M. Kahn, "SOM's Sensible Shelters," *Wall Street Journal,* August 31, 1992.
9. Camilo José Vergara, "New York's New Ghettos," *The Nation,* June 17, 1991, 804.
10. Jan Hoffman, "Rebuilding Lives While Reviving Buildings," *Metro,* March 3, 2000.
11. Personal correspondence with Beyer Blinder Belle, November 15, 2002.
12. Charles V. Bagli, "As Landlords Howl, Giuliani Supports Prince George Plan," *New York Observer,* December 26, 1994–January 2, 1995.

ILLUSTRATION CREDITS

Figures 1, 2, 3	Photographs © Barbara White
Figure 4	KMA Architecture & Engineering
Figure 5	St. Vincent de Paul Village
Figure 6	Photograph: Davis & Joyce Architects
Figure 7	Photograph: Ed Glendinning
Figure 8	Courtesy of Scott MacGillivray Architects
Figures 9, 10, 11	Nadel Architects
Figure 12	Drawing by Dorothée Imbert for Paul Groth
Figure 13	Photograph: Paul Groth
Figures 14, 15	Architects: Marguerite McGoldrick and Gans + Jelacic. Photographs: Nathaniel H. Brooks/Van Alen Institute, New York.
Figure 16	Drawing by Dorothée Imbert for Paul Groth
Figure 17	Rob Wellington Quigley, FAIA
Figures 18, 19	Koning Isenberg Architects. Photographs: Benny Chan/Fotoworks.
Figure 20	Donald MacDonald Architect. Photograph: Joshua Freiwald (joshuafreiwald.com).
Figure 21	Photograph: Clay Davis
Figure 22	Photograph © Paul Fusco/Magnum Photos
Figures 23, 24	Photographs: Sam Davis
Figure 25	The Philips + Fotheringham Partnership
Figure 26	Photograph: Elmer W. J. Frey
Figure 27	Architect: Moshe Safdie. Photograph: Sam Davis.
Figure 28	Photograph: Jim Reid
Figure 29	Redrawn from HabitatfortheHomeless.com. Jim Reid, designer.
Figure 30	Courtesy of the Bancroft Library, University of California, Berkeley
Figure 31	Architect: Herman & Coliver. Photograph: Sam Davis.
Figure 32	Sam Davis
Figure 33	Davis & Joyce Architects
Figure 34	Architect: Asian Neighborhood Design. Photograph © Mark Citret.
Figure 35	Sam Davis Architecture. Photograph © Russell Abraham 2002.
Figure 36	Sam Davis Architecture
Figure 37	Architect: Skidmore, Owings, & Merrill, LLP. Photograph © T. Whitney Cox.
Figure 38	Architect: Asian Neighborhood Design. Photograph © Mark Citret.
Figure 39	Davis & Joyce Architects
Figure 40	Davis & Joyce Architects.

Figure 40	Photograph © Russell Abraham 2002.
Figure 41	Sam Davis Architecture. Photograph © Russell Abraham 2002.
Figures 42, 43	Sam Davis Architecture
Figures 44, 45	Redrawn by permission of Gran Associates Architects & Planners, LLC (formerly Gran-Sultan Associates)
Figures 46, 47	Gran Associates Architects & Planners, LLC (formerly Gran-Sultan Associates)
Figure 48	Davis & Joyce Architects. Rendering: Kevin Kodama.
Figure 49	Davis & Joyce Architects. Photograph: Carolyn Greis.
Figure 50	Davis & Joyce Architects
Figure 51	Architects: Errol Barron/Michael Toups. Photograph: Toby Armstrong.
Figure 52	Architects: Errol Barron/Michael Toups
Figure 53	Davis & Joyce Architects
Figures 54, 55	Davis & Joyce Architects. Photograph © Russell Abraham 2002.
Figures 56, 57, 58	Jeffrey M. Kalban & Associates Architecture, Inc.
Figures 59, 60	Herman & Coliver Architects. Photographs: Mark Luthringer.
Figures 61, 62	Herman & Coliver Architects
Figures 63, 64, 65	Skidmore, Owings & Merrill, LLP
Figures 66, 67	Skidmore, Owings & Merrill, LLP. Photograph © T. Whitney Cox.
Figure 68	Skidmore, Owings & Merrill, LLP
Figure 69	Beyer Blinder Belle Architects and Planners, LLP
Figure 70	Photograph: Deborah Samuelson; courtesy Common Ground Community
Figure 71	Photograph: Joe Vericker/Photobureau; courtesy Common Ground Community
Figures 72, 73	Beyer Blinder Belle Architects and Planners, LLP. Photographs: Joe Vericker/Photobureau.
Figure 74	Photograph: Joe Vericker/Photobureau; courtesy Common Ground Community
Figure 75	Beyer Blinder Belle Architects and Planners, LLP. Photograph: Joe Vericker/Photobureau.

INDEX

Page numbers in italics refer to illustrations.

ACQUISITIONS EDITORS: *James Clark, Stephanie Fay*
ASSISTANT ACQUISITIONS EDITOR: *Erin Marietta*
PROJECT EDITOR: *Sue Heinemann*
EDITORIAL ASSISTANT: *Lynn Meinhardt*
COPYEDITOR: *Charles Dibble*
INDEXER: *Ruth Elwell*
DESIGNER: *Victoria Kuskowski*
PRODUCTION COORDINATOR: *John Cronin*
TEXT: *9.75/14 Sabon*
DISPLAY: *Grotesque MT BL*
COMPOSITOR: *Integrated Composition Systems*
PRINTER + BINDER: *Thomson-Shore*